MAKE MUSIC!

A KID'S GUIDE to Creating Rhythm, Playing with Sound, and Conducting and Composing Music

Norma Jean Haynes,
Ann Sayre Wiseman, and
John Langstaff

Storey Publishing

*The mission of Storey Publishing is to serve our customers by
publishing practical information that encourages
personal independence in harmony with the environment.*

Edited by Deborah Burns
Art direction and book design by Alethea Morrison
Prop styling and text production by Liseann Karandisecky
Indexed by Samantha Miller

Cover photography by Mars Vilaubi, except back, center, and author
     photo by © Jared Leeds Photography
Location photography by © Jared Leeds Photography
Studio photography by Mars Vilaubi
Additional photography credits below

Illustrations by © Jessica Gibson
Wooden instrument construction by Tony Pisano
Score on page 120 by Yeshe Gutschow Rai, age 10

Text © 2019 Storey Publishing, LLC, except for additional musical text
and creative teaching methods including Clock Music, Playing the
Room, Paper Orchestra, and Soundscapes © 2003 John Langstaff

Portions of this book previously appeared in *Making Music* by Ann
Sayre Wiseman and John Langstaff (Storey Publishing, 2003).

The bar measurements on page 112 are reprinted from *Musical
Instruments Made to Be Played* by Ronald Roberts, published by Dryad
Press, Woodridge, New Jersey. Storey Publishing was unable to locate
the owner of the copyright and would welcome that person's contact
information.

Storey Publishing
210 MASS MoCA Way
North Adams, MA 01247
storey.com

Printed in China by Printplus Ltd.
10 9 8 7 6 5 4 3 2 1

Library of Congress Cataloging-in-Publication Data on file

Additional photography by:
© 101cats/iStock.com, 16 balloon; © Africa media Online/Alamy
Stock Photo, 37 right; © akinshin/iStock.com, 48 milk carton; ©
AlexStar/iStock.com, 62 apple; © Anthony DOUANNE/iStock.com, 62
pear; © BamBamImages/iStock.com, 16 door; © baona/iStock.com,
127 bottom; © BLOOMimage/Getty Images, 22; © Carol Yepes/
Getty Images, 125; © Catherine Ledner/Getty Images, 21 monkey;
© The Estate of David Gahr/Getty Images, 68 Bessie Jones; ©
ddukang/iStock.com, 88 acoustic guitar; © Dinodia Photos/Alamy
Stock Photo, 28 jal tarang; © DmitriyKazitsyn/iStock.com, 34 mug;
© Editorial Image Provider/Getty Images, 120; © EfsunKutlay/
iStock.com, 52 grater; © Eric Schaal/Getty Images, 67 John Cage;
© filipfoto/iStock.com, 132; © Floortje/iStock.com, 123 xylophone;
© GeorgePeters/iStock.com, 81 acorns; © GlobalP/iStock.com,
16 chipmunk; © Grassetto/iStock.com, 16 refrigerator; © Hulton
Collection/Getty Images, 89; © idealistock/iStock.com, 122 drum;
© JamesPearsell/iStock.com, 84; © JoKMedia/iStock.com, 18 ball;
© KariHoglund/iStock.com, 123 rattles; Kasimir Malewicz, Stedelijk
Museum, Amsterdam/Wikimedia Commons, 85; © Kovaleva_Ka/
iStock.com, 62 pineapple; © ksushsh/iStock.com, 82 flowers;

© Life On White/Getty Images, 21 lion; © Linghe Zhao/Getty
Images, 96; © Mark Kauffman/Getty Images, 34 Benjamin Britten;
© mbongorus/iStock.com, 23 gong; © M Swiet Productions/
Getty Images, 20; © Nadezhda1906/iStock.com, 135; © perets/
iStock.com, 123 trumpet; © Pictorial Press Ltd./Alamy Stock Photo,
124; © PIUS UTOMI EKPEI/Getty Images, 66; © RG-vc/iStock.com,
126 microphone; © Robert Hamm/Alamy Stock Photo, 106 bottom;
© Roman_Gorielov/iStock.com, 115 bottom; © Serg_Velusceac/
iStock.com, 48 gourds; © seyfettinozel/iStock.com, 29 glasses;
© Siri Stafford/Getty Images, 133; © skynesher/iStock.com, 18 horse;
© stickytoffeepudding/iStock.com, 34 whisk; © Svisho/iStock.com,
65; © tarasov_vl/iStock.com, 16 violin; © THEERADECH SANIN/
iStock.com, 16 bottle; © Thomas Barwick/Getty Images, 19; © Thomas
Northcut/Getty Image, 21 dog; © tiler84/iStock.com, 88 electric
guitar; © TPopova/iStock.com, 34 pot; © Tuned_In/Getty Images, 127
top; © ValentynVolkov/iStock.com, 62 plum; © Vassiliy Vishnevskiy/
iStock.com, 130; © wildpixel/iStock.com, 44 zipper; © windy55/
iStock.com, 29 spoon; © xxmmxx/iStock.com, 52 spatula; © YinYang/
iStock.com, 126 leaves; © ZargonDesign/iStock.com, 122 guitar

Music belongs to **everyone**.

— Gunnar Schonbeck,
instrument inventor and teacher

Contents

Breath Music
The Winds
71

The String Section
87

Instruments from the Workshop
105

Creating Music
119

Beginning Notes

From Norma Jean Haynes

If I could offer one piece of wisdom for the new musician — and at age 21, I am a newish musician myself — it would be this:

Follow your ears.

Just days after my 20th birthday, I heard the most incredible music wafting down the street in Paris, France. I followed the sound to an unmarked storefront, where a door swung open on friends laughing and eating around a table. A woman sang by a piano, and unfamiliar musical instruments hung on the walls: inflatable blue guitars and pointy, shimmery metal structures. My ears had led me to the studio of the Baschet brothers, two renowned inventors of musical instruments.

The friends saw me and invited me in. Hesitating, I asked myself a question, one that would reappear months later, when I was invited to contribute to this book:

Who makes the music in our world? Is it the conductor before a hushed orchestra? Is it the pop star with billions of YouTube views, or a mother rocking her baby to sleep with a lullaby? Maybe it's the cat, wailing for his supper. Could it be **you**?

"Oh no, not me — I'm not a musician!"

For 20 years, Ann Wiseman and John Langstaff's book *Making Music* has insisted that music is expansive enough to include everyone. All that is required is the intent to listen.

Follow your ears! Our world is filled to the brim with sound: the *murmur* of talk radio, the *tut-puddle-trickle-purrr* of the coffeemaker, the *ra-ra-ta-tum* of the cash register. In the 21st century, we live in a constant soundscape, yet it is easy to take sound for granted, forgetting our right to participate. In *Make Music!* creative listening is a gateway to creative participation: we stop, we listen, we make our own contribution to the world's orchestra.

Increasingly, music is recognized as a tool to collaborate and communicate across divides of culture and language, regardless of resources and materials available. In the new edition, I've included stories and perspectives on how music is used in diverse communities as a part of daily life and work. I hope that you, your family, your students, and your friends might find the ways that it fits into yours.

So jump in! Enjoy discovering the sounds around you, learning (and sometimes ignoring) basic principles of musical structure, and traveling the musical map through an exploration of homemade instruments.

Ann Sayre Wiseman and John "Jack" Langstaff, the two authors of an earlier version of this book, were artists, performers, and passionate teachers. Ann is responsible for most of the instrument-building projects, and John for many musical games and activities.

From Ann Sayre Wiseman

Whenever I hear that music, art, and creativity are being cut from the school budget, that learning by doing is being eliminated from the curriculum, I write books to show that creativity is the best and most long-lasting way to learn about life, facts, truths, how things are made, and how things work.

Creativity does not require a special budget or special teachers; it requires imagination, common sense, and resourcefulness. Time to explore should be a basic part of all teaching and learning. When the hands can make something that works, the body is delighted, the mind is validated, and immediately you become a teacher yourself who can pass the skill on to someone else who wants to learn.

Improvising musical instruments is an excellent way to encourage creative thinking, and nature has given us amazing sounds as examples. You can find rhythm and sound everywhere: the wind blowing through trees and whistling over holes, thunder in the sky, waves on the sand, rivers rushing by, rain drumming the roof. Singing, humming, slapping, clapping, tapping — wonderful sounds, a scale of notes, free of charge.

We have made instruments that copy these natural sounds. A gourd strung with a sinew or vine makes a crying sound. Almost anything can be used as a drum. Blowing through reeds makes different notes.

When I was working at Boston Children's Museum, I took a group of kids to the dump with a wooden spoon in each hand to collect good sounds. Car parts were the best. We then went to our kitchens and tapped pots, pans, everything we could hang from strings. We blew into pipes and reeds. We collected sounds for our DAM GOOD DUMP BAND, and you can, too. Hang your sounds from a fence, a shelf, a rack, or the branches of a tree. Invite your friends to come and make music, compose a symphony, write a score.

From John Langstaff

The little girl stood thinking, motionless, in the middle of the room, facing a semicircle of children holding improvised instruments, and contemplated how she might begin the music.

Looking over her attentive "orchestra," she slowly raised her arm and suddenly pointed to one player. The whirring, metallic sound of an eggbeater began quietly, growing slightly in volume as the conductor's other hand beckoned pitched notes plucked at random from a kalimba — dozens of little notes shimmering over the low drone. Eventually she introduced a different texture, seeds in a large gourd shaken to a furious crescendo. Next, she coolly pointed to a child clasping two large pot lids, which he clashed together as primitive cymbals. Now the young conductor fervently waved her arms, luring the players on and indicating the entrance of the remaining musicians.

At this point there was a density of sound in which I could hear a xylophone, notes of a recorder, and a single drum making a continuous pattern underneath it all. As the cacophony rose to a climax, the conductor held up one hand to signal the clanging, dominating pot lids to cease. Suddenly she held both hands above her head, focusing her players, and then her arms shot down, outstretched, and abruptly cut the music off.

The silence was stunning — but only for a moment. To my surprise, the young conductor-composer's hand flew out to cue in again the original first instruments. I heard the low growl of the eggbeater joined by the sparkling notes of the kalimba, just the two quiet instruments continuing on and on . . . until she wiped them out with a pass of her hand to end the piece.

I was fascinated. Her music ended as it had started. Here was a very young "composer" fashioning a score right on the spot, as she conducted her orchestra of homemade instruments for the first time — dealing with the same problems Beethoven had. **How to begin? Where to go, and how to get there? How to end?**

This is the essence of making music together, and it can be experienced using homemade instruments, as described in this book. Children have a natural affinity to rhythm, and this book offers ways to get them immediately involved. As they become more and more engaged in improvising with their instruments, they learn about basic musical elements such as tempo, dynamics, phrasing, and polyrhythms. As they create their own compositions, they naturally learn how to shape them.

Presented effectively, this musicmaking is like a fascinating game to children — and to adults as well. Entire families can have musical fun together. Let's begin!

A Little Note on Technology

Ladies and gentlemen, please silence your cell phones now!

Modern technology is changing the ways we make, share, and build community around music. What else in our lives makes sound besides recordings — and *how*?

Human beings have made music together for thousands of years, but they have been sitting alone in front of computers for less than a hundred.

The projects and activities of this book ask us to work, play, and move together, gloriously face-to-face.

Once you've spent some time exploring the musical possibilities of your body and surroundings, then use technology as support. Check out videos of musicians around the world online, or use a device to record (see page 125) your compositions.

Body Music

Listen to your heartbeat — it's also called a *pulse*. You can find it by touching two fingers to your wrist or to either side of your neck. Feel that little *pa-dum, pa-dum, pa-dum*? That's the rhythm of your body working: slow or fast, it's your heart drumming... from the first to the last.

Why not march to the beat of your own drummer, and learn the ways your body can make music? This chapter will help you slap, snap, and clap your way to the music of your choice.

CLAPPING AND BODY DRUMMING

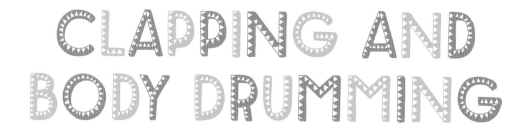

Were hands, voice, and feet our first instruments? Hands can make different sounds depending on how you put them together.

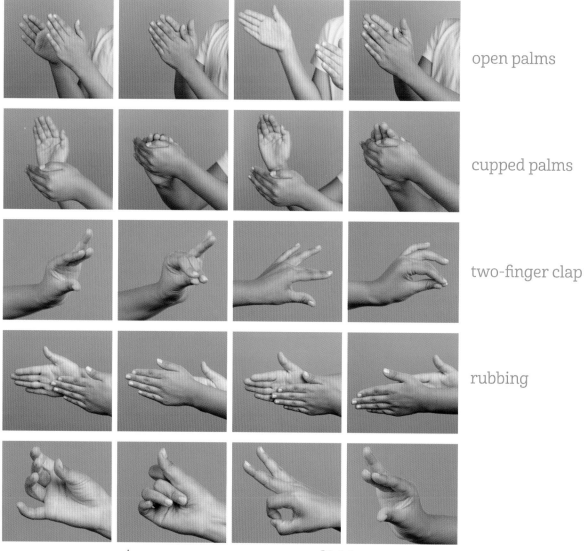

open palms

cupped palms

two-finger clap

rubbing

snapping

flicking

West Africans who were brought to the United States as slaves used drums to share messages in rhythmic codes. When their drums were taken away by slaveowners, they used **body drumming** — stomping their feet; patting their cheeks full of air; slapping their arms, chest, and legs — to communicate.

"**Hambone**" or "**Juba dance**," as this body music was called, kept African rhythms alive in the United States. Those rhythms are at the heart of American music, from jazz to hip-hop. Dances like tap dancing and stepping, an African-American style developed by college students, were influenced by these African rhythms and the body-drumming tradition.

An easy hambone pattern goes like this:

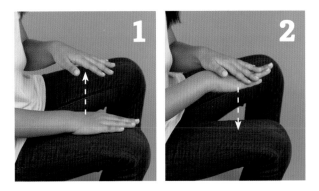

1. Hold one hand above your knee, palm down. Place the other hand on your knee. Bring it up to slap your palm.
2. Let the moving hand bounce between your knee and your palm. Try this pattern: *knee-palm-knee, knee-palm-knee, knee-palm-knee, knee-palm-knee.*

Can you hear the low sound, or **pitch**, of the knee slap, and the higher pitch of the palm slap?

stepping

Body Drumming

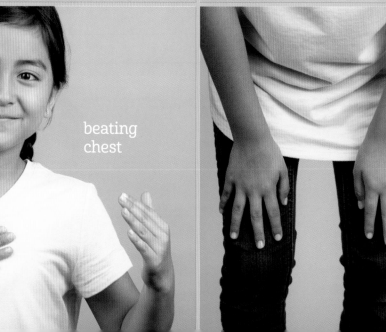

patting cheeks full of air

clicking heels

tapping toes

beating chest

slapping thighs

Clock Music Opus 1
BODY BOP

A score is a piece of music written out for several people to play together. A clock face makes a great base for writing a musical score. It works for a solo player or several players, each choosing a different part. You will need a real clock with a second hand, which will be your conductor. As the clock ticks, each tick is **one beat**.

Study the list of sounds. Choose your favorite! Find on the clock score when that sound is to be played.

▧ = rubbing palms together

▲ = clicking tongue

● = snapping fingers

★ = humming

◆ = whistling (any notes)

◗ = clapping

✳ = stamping feet

(no symbol) = silence

⚇ = yell

The word **opus** (meaning "creative work" in Latin) is used to keep a composer's works in order. Opus 1 is his or her first piece, Opus 2 the second, and so on. What will your Opus 1 sound like?

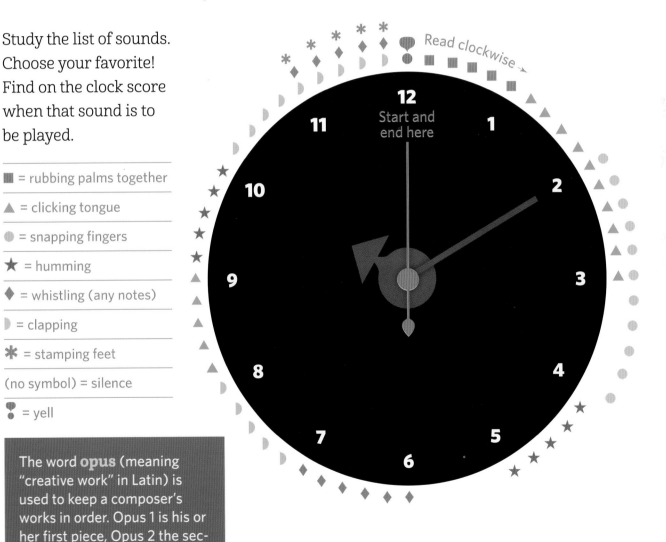

USING YOUR VOICE

Explore the **sonic** (sound-making) possibilities of your voice.
Can you make the sound of:

A door
creaking

A violin

The hum of a
refrigerator

A chipmunk

Air escaping
from a soda
bottle

What is the loudest sound
you can make? ↑

The softest? ↓

The roundest? O

Record yourself
making these sounds,
and play them back.

Use your voice to tell a
story. Sing the journey of
a balloon disappearing in
the high sky.

Imagine a lump
of peanut butter
is stuck in your
mouth. Try to
sing a song while
chewing the
imaginary peanut
butter. Record these
sounds, too!

The human **voice** is the most delightful, versatile **instrument** — yet it has no weight.

Rhythms and Rhymes

Rhythm is the repeating pulse of a jump rope slapping the ground, of water dripping from a faucet, of a swing swaying back and forth. Each time the rope hits the floor, a water drop falls, or your feet brush the ground is one beat.

Rhyme is the matching of a word's sound.

A song usually has both rhythm and rhyme. Sing your favorite song while swinging or bouncing a ball. How does your song fit with your movement?

Not all music has a regular beat: a horse trots, then gallops, then slows to a stop. Its rhythmic hooves move the horse from one place to another. In a similar way, rhythm carries music through time.

You can make the clip-clop sound of a horse's hooves with two coconut halves.

Jump Rope Chants

Here are some simple spoken chants to go with jump rope or clapping patterns. See if your friends or classmates know any others.

This one comes from very old English:

Onery, orey ickery Ann
Phyllison, Phollison, Nichols Jan
Queevy, Quavy, English Navy
Tinklum, tanklum, tee taw buck

This one is more modern American:

Fudge, fudge, call the judge.
Mama's got a newborn baby.
Wrap it up in tissue paper,
Send it down the elevator.
How many babies
Will Mama have?
1, 2, 3, 4, 5,
6, 7, 8, 9, 10!

Animal Sounds

How long have humans been imitating animal sounds? Forever, probably.

Mosquitos buzz! Say the word *buzz* and hold onto the *zzz* sound for as long as you can. Push the air out hard between your tongue and teeth, and get ready for it to tickle.

A lion's roar is challenging to mimic with your voice. I think it sounds like a big yawn, or maybe snorting gently through your nose while breathing in.

Humpback whales also make marvelous sounds: they purr, moo, groan, and bellow. What we call "whalesong" and "birdsong" may simply be animals speaking to one another. Of course, we humans communicate through music, too!

Try This

With your friends, create an animal choir. Each person chooses a different animal to mimic. Try singing all together, in small groups, or with animal solos and duets. How, for instance, would a dog sing "Amazing Grace"?

And of course, don't forget the birds. Composers have always been inspired by birdcalls: their rhythms and melodies. Some birds can shift quickly between pitches or even sing two notes at once. That's hard for humans to copy, but musicians try anyway!

Some composers include birdsong in their compositions. Clarinetist David Rothenberg actually plays his own invented melodies to birds — and sometimes they sing back!

Whistling

Make your lips into the tiniest possible ⭕ shape. Rest your tongue behind your bottom teeth.

Blow out a narrow stream of air very softly, as if you are blowing out a tiny birthday candle. Keep your lips tight, and listen for the sound.

Blow a little **harder** to make a **louder** sound.

Try whistling different **pitches**.

Try whistling as you **breathe sharply in**. How does it sound and feel different from when you blow out?

Now whistle a tune!

Resonance

Have you ever struck a bell or a gong and noticed how it shakes for a long time? That's called **resonating**. Our bodies resonate when we sing, and you can make many interesting sounds by using your voice and tapping your body at the same time.

Make your mouth into an O, and tap your palm over your mouth while you sing.

Gently thump your chest while you sing. How is it different with your hands flat, or in fists?

Hold your nose while you sing for a funny stuffy sound.

Covering your ears will change how you sound to yourself — but not to others. Try cupping your hands over your ears, then uncovering them.

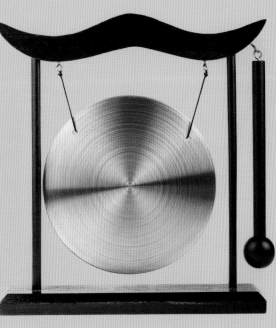

This is a gong. When you strike it with a mallet, the sound **resonates** through the instrument, the floor, the room, and everyone in it!

Name Games

Each name has its own music. Say your name out loud, slowly. Keep repeating it until you forget what it means. How does it sound?

CHLO-e
CHLO-e
CHLO-e
CHLO-e
CHLO-e
CHLO-e

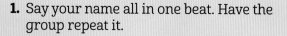

1. Say your name all in one beat. Have the group repeat it.

2. Go around the circle with the group echoing each name.

3. Then repeat your own name in one beat, over and over, with other players adding their names.

4. Listen as the rhythms pile up.

5. Now play your names, two or three at a time, with body drumming or percussion instruments.

6. Listen to the different patterns: these are called polyrhythms.

A-ME-li-a
UR-su-la
NOR-ma-JEAN
LO-re-lei
E-than
Na-TA-sha
Lise-ANN
JAR-ed
DEB
SU-per-man
E-LIZ-a-beth
Ta-SHAI

Household Things

That Ring and Ping

Many surprising things — when hung from strings — begin to sing! Kitchen utensils, recycled containers, and all manner of objects resonate when tapped. Here are some instruments you can play this way.

BELLS & CHIMES

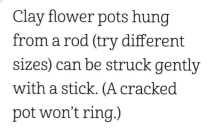

Clay flower pots hung from a rod (try different sizes) can be struck gently with a stick. (A cracked pot won't ring.)

Ceramic bowls filled with different amounts of water are like an ancient Indian instrument, *jal tarang*. Tap gently with a stick or wooden spoon.

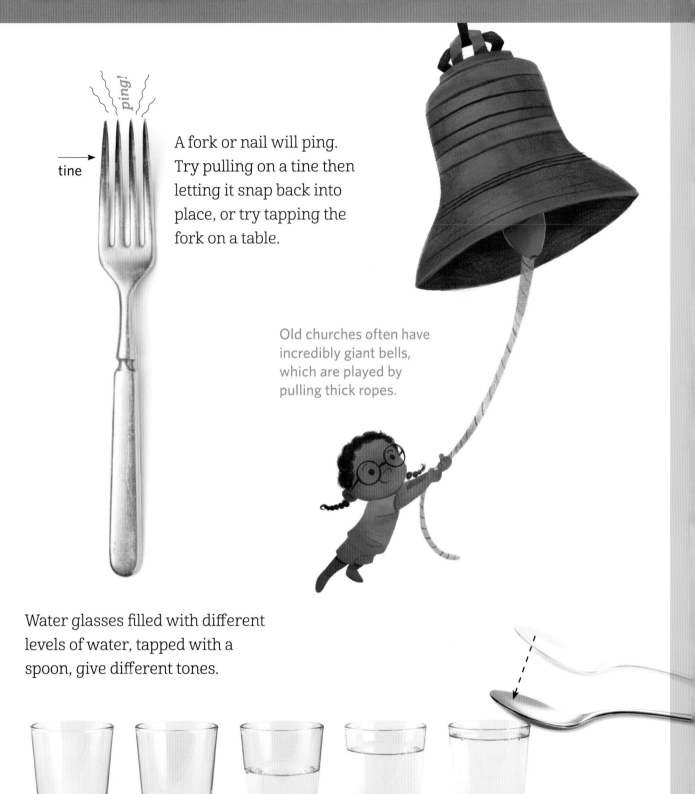

ping!

tine

A fork or nail will ping. Try pulling on a tine then letting it snap back into place, or try tapping the fork on a table.

Old churches often have incredibly giant bells, which are played by pulling thick ropes.

Water glasses filled with different levels of water, tapped with a spoon, give different tones.

Triangles

A bent steel bar, suspended, can make the sound of a triangle. A metal striker, like a screwdriver or a steel fork or spoon, will bring forth the best sound.

The triangle is an important part of Cajun music in Louisiana, where it's played along with the fiddle and accordion. The Cajuns are descended from French settlers, and they call the triangle a *'tit fer* (tee fair) after the French *petit fer* — "little iron."

To play like the Cajuns, hang the triangle on your thumb or index finger, and open and close your fingers around the bar to dampen the sound. Hear the two different notes?

Cajun style: open hand

Cajun style: closed hand

Coat Hanger Chimes

Want to privately hear a most amazing sound of big, tolling bells?

1. Take an unpainted metal coat hanger and a yard-long piece of string.

2. Wind the middle of the string around the hanger hook.

3. Wrap the ends of the string around your index fingers, and then stick your fingers in your ears.

4. Lean forward so the hanger swings freely enough to strike an object — chair, table, and so on.

5. Listen.

You can attach more strings to the coat hanger so that several people can hear the bells at the same time!

Dong! Dong! Dong!

Mallets

Felt, rubber, or wood; big or small; soft or hard; mallets come in many shapes and sizes.

Thread spool on a stick

Section of coat hanger carefully pushed into a cork
(an adult can use a nail file, or emery board, to dull sharp wires)

Pencil with eraser as the beater

Dowel pushed into an old tennis ball,
perfect for striking a gong — ask an adult for help

Dowel or chopstick with rubber bands or strips of inner tubing

Pencil with metal nut for striking metal

Large knitting needle

A mallet has a head; a drumstick does not.
For drumstick ideas, see page 60.

KITCHEN CONCERTO

Hang household things on strings, and strike them with mallets. (See page 33 for some ideas for mallets.) With a parent's help, make an outdoor "installation" (setup), or hang small things on a meterstick or yardstick between two chairs.

Tap everything. See what rings, pings, and sings! Play the kitchen grate and scrape. Make up a piece for five kitchen instruments and two moments of silence.

Benjamin Britten used mugs tuned to different pitches and hung from strings in his children's opera *Noye's Fludde* (based on the Biblical story of Noah). He called these "slung mugs." The player struck them with a wooden spoon to create the sound of the first raindrops hitting the boat in the story of Noah's Ark.

A number of composers have written music for **kitchen utensils**, including Henry Brant, who wrote a piece called *Kitchen Music* in 1946.

MUSICAL CLOTHING

With a few stitches and pins, your clothes can become musical instruments.

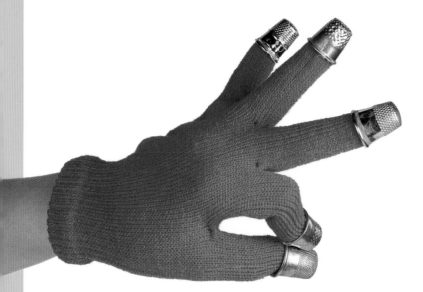

Sew buttons on your old gloves,
or glue on thimbles to make
Thimble Fingers.

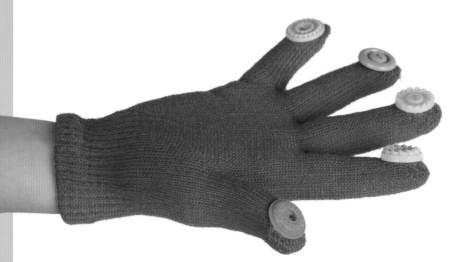

Glue pennies or tie some
washers to the bottoms
of your old shoes: instant
tap shoes!

Sew bells onto ribbons, like the Morris dancers of England, or use metal jingles.

Gumboot dancer in South Africa

In South Africa, mine workers make rhythms using the sounds of their galoshes (also known as gumboots). Slapping the sides of your boots makes a great sound; so does stomping on the ground. Try a combination of the two. (Rain puddles are fun, but not required!)

POT COVER CYMBALS

Clash, ring, and ping!

Small lids = high tones

Large lids = low tones

Tap outside edge with pencil. Find the best tones.

Tap with fingernails or Thimble Fingers (see page 36).

Unscrew knobs from covers. Thread string through holes. Use thread spools, knots, or buttons to allow space between the lids.

American composer Kenneth Frazelle wrote a piece for pots and pans called "Shivaree."

Do you know what a "shivaree" is? It's a noisy, raucous parade that occurs around Europe and in Canada and the United States. People play pot-and-pan drums and howl like alley cats to embarrass somebody.

Imagine a shivaree coming to your door. Yikes!

Clock Music Opus 2
A LITTLE PIECE FOR TWO POT COVERS

Here is a clock score for a solo player or several on different parts. You need a real clock with a second hand, which will be your conductor. For this piece, you will use two pot covers, a fork, the clock score, and the real clock.

■ = Tap with fork

▲ = Scratch and scrape with fork

● = Strike with fork

🍴 = Loud bang with fork

(no symbol) = Silence

◗ = Flick pot rim with fingernail

◆ = Knock with knuckles

✳ = Drum your fingernails

✖ = Slowly grind together two pot covers

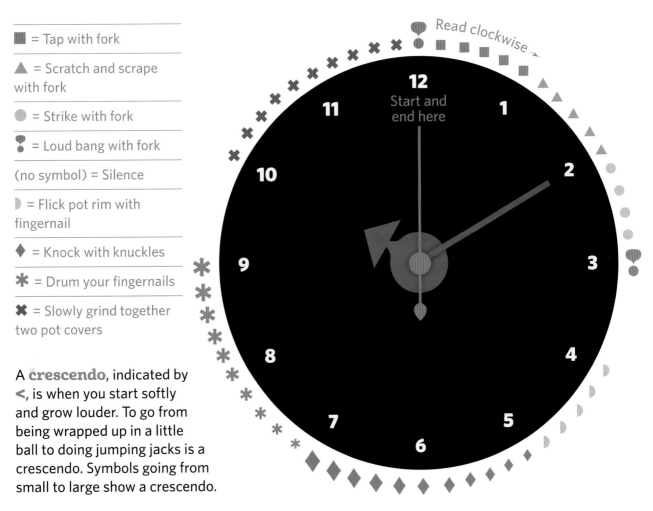

Read clockwise →

Start and end here

A **crescendo**, indicated by <, is when you start softly and grow louder. To go from being wrapped up in a little ball to doing jumping jacks is a crescendo. Symbols going from small to large show a crescendo.

A **diminuendo**, indicated by >, is the opposite: you start loud and grow soft. This can be like starting with jumping jacks and winding up in a ball. Symbols going from large to small show a diminuendo.

Crying Water Bowls & Cooking Pots

Pots and pans ring and sing when struck. Swirling water distorts the notes and carries the sound. Take a stainless-steel bowl. Swirl ½ cup of water around. Strike it on the bottom to hear a strange sound! John remembers English children striking a cymbal and lowering it into a bucket of water, producing a fantastic roar.

Swish the water
and tap the bottom.

Chinese composer Tan Dun composed a piece called *Water Concerto,* which combines the different sounds of water with a full orchestra. The piece celebrates the beauty of water and its many uses, but for Tan Dun it also expresses sadness at how much water is polluted on Earth.

Glass Harmonica

You can make clear pitches from thin-rimmed glasses of water filled to different levels. Wet one of your fingers. Rub it around the glass rim until the sound begins. Try playing a song.

Benjamin Franklin loved this pure clear sound and built an instrument to make it easier to produce. He called it the Glass Armonica. He composed his own pieces for the instrument and traveled through Europe performing on it.

Foot pedals rotated a series of glass bowls of increasing sizes set in a trough of water. When a finger touched the moist, spinning bowl, it produced a clear musical tone.

Mozart liked the sound of the glass harmonica so much that he wrote several compositions for it, and Beethoven wrote one, too.

More recently, experimental composer Meredith Monk released a whole album of compositions for a singing voice and a glass of water, called *Our Lady of Late*.

41

CONDUCTING AN ORCHESTRA

Choose someone to be the conductor, to decide which instrument should be played when.

Before beginning, the conductor has to listen to each instrument to know its sound. Each sound is like a color. There must be absolute silence at the start, just like a blank canvas. Then the conductor points to the first sound and starts to paint a picture with music.

How can you move your hands to show loud and soft sounds? Growing (crescendo) and shrinking (diminuendo) sounds?

Point to others to bring them in, combine different sounds, thin them out. Make moments of magical silence. Conduct the orchestra to an ending.

Take turns as conductor. Record a performance (page 125) and play it back later.

In Vienna, Austria, there is an orchestra called the Vegetable Orchestra, with instruments made only from vegetables. Leftover vegetable pieces are cooked into soup for the audience!

Velcro~Zipper Duets

Zippers and Velcro on jackets and shoes
zapped and **zipped** make sounds you
can use for a jazzy duet.

Make up a composition:
short and long strokes,
fast and slow, solo
and together. Create
patterns — talk back
and forth.

Use a duffel bag or
sleeping bag zipper to
make a long, slow sound.

Paper Ensemble

Give each player sheets of newspaper, a magazine, or a small paper bag. **LISTEN** as you rip, tear, rattle, shake, crumple, twist, snap, and flap the paper — and then pop a whole paper bag with a final bang. Take turns conducting.

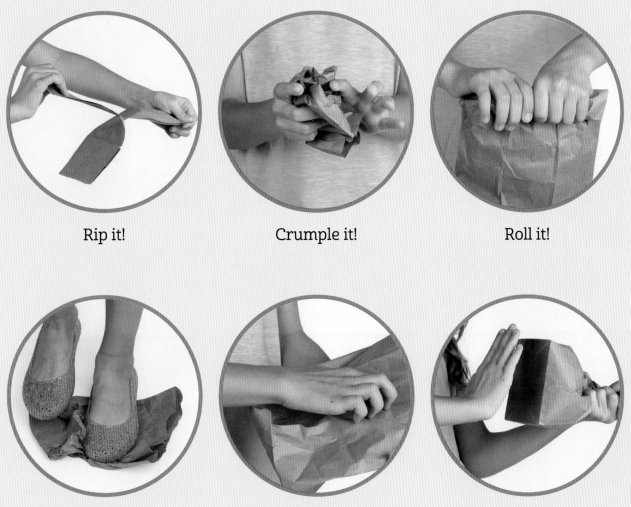

Rip it!   Crumple it!   Roll it!

Stomp on it!   Scrape it!   Pop it!

Percussion
Beats and Rhythms

When in doubt, drum! Percussion instruments are made of many materials. Ancient drums and rattles were made of wood, clay, and animal hide. Modern ones can be made out of plastic and recycled materials. Let the materials you have guide you.

Maracas
RATTLE & CLATTER

Use any empty container: plastic, wood, paper, glass, or cardboard, filled with stones, rice, beans, peas, or sand. Make two, and shake one in each hand.

Fill a **plastic lemon** with rice or seeds and slide it on a chopstick.

Keys on a string rattle.

Seeds inside a **gourd** will rattle when dry.

Scallop or clam shells can be clamped together. Ask an adult to split a dowel tip to hold the shells. Put tiny pebbles in the shells. Attach with a strong elastic, string, or shoelace.

Fill a small or large **milk carton** with pebbles, lentils, buttons, or other small items.

To make a shaker, insert four or five paper clips or a jingle bell into a **balloon** *before* you blow it up.

Two **paper soup bowls** or **aluminum pie pans** rattle when glued together with pebbles inside.

A shaker has two sounds:

Back beat

Forward beat

For a clear, short sound, pretend you're hitting a drumhead with your maracas. Stop the motion with a flick of the wrist.

CASTANETS & CLAPPERS

Bottle caps attached to thumb and finger with Band-Aids or cloth or paper loops make good castanets.

To make **walnut castanets**, tape cloth or cardboard finger loops onto empty shells. Use only good shells — a crack will spoil the tone. Or try acorns on your fingers.

In parts of Spain, women take shells from the beach to use as castanets and then dance while clicking them. You can also scrape the backs of two scallop shells together.

Jar lids with safety buttons, like those found on tomato sauce jars, jam jars, and iced tea or coffee in glass bottles, make cricket or popping sounds when pressed at the center. Or make castanets using a whole array of safety button lids!

Buttons, glued onto a strip of cardboard, make a tiny clicking sound.

Pinch the cardboard sides to click the buttons.

Spoons, wood or metal, clapped together, make a good hollow sound. Try holding two spoons, the backs of their scoops touching, with a finger or two in between. Grip tight, and hit between your other palm and your knee.

SCRAPERS & RASPS

Scrapers produce an intriguing, long percussive tone: like a cat stretching its spine. Rasps have ridges or prickly points and they buzz or click or tick when scraped.

Look around the kitchen!

Strum a metal pancake flipper.

Scrape a cheese grater with a stick, a plastic pen, or Thimble Fingers (see page 36).

Accordion-fold a sheet of thin cardboard, like the front of a cereal box, and stroke it with a spoon.

Run a pencil along the bumps of an egg carton.

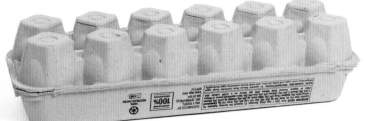

Sand Blocks

Glue or tack sandpaper onto wooden blocks. Tack on tape or ribbon as handholds. Scratch the blocks back and forth to play.

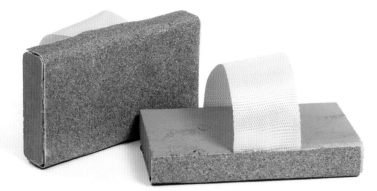

The Guiro

The guiro is a Latin American instrument, traditionally made from a dry, bumpy gourd or even a bone. Ours is made from a stick, but feel free to notch a gourd if you have one on hand.

Notch a twig or pencil and scrape it with a stick or slightly bent wire for strumming. Use a box, a bowl, or a pot for a **sounding board**. A sounding board will help your instrument resonate.

A Pre-Hispanic Orchestra

The earliest instruments created in Central and South America date back to 8000 BCE, and they are the great-grandparents of many instruments played today. Drums made of hollow tree trunks and tortoise shells, whistles made from clay and gourds, and single-stringed instruments were all played thousands of years ago by Native people.

Wooden rainsticks in many shapes, often that of a snake

Seedpod rattles

Gourd drum

Claves & Rhythm Sticks

The clave keeps the beat for Afro-Cuban music. Use 1"-diameter hardwood dowels, 4" or 5" long.

The lower clave must rest *on* your fist, so the cradle of your fingers and thumb can act as a sounding box (see page 88). (Holding the dowel *in* your fist will deaden the sound.)

MAKE-DO DRUMS

Make a bass drum that can be played on both sides. Tie a cardboard or plastic box around your stomach. Attach an egg carton to the front for a scraper.

In many Native American traditions, the drum sound represents a **heartbeat**.

Fabric covered with white glue makes a good drumhead — the glue will dry, tightening the drumhead. Rubber bed sheets, layered balloons, and inner tubing will also work.

A **coconut**, **gourd**, or **wooden vessel** can have plastic, cloth, leather, or chamois stretched over tightly, glued underneath, and tied.

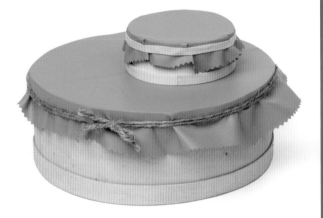

Make different sizes!

Other Easy Ideas

A **coffee can** with a plastic lid on one end or both makes a quick drum.

Turn an empty plastic **milk jug** upside down.

Use a cardboard **ice cream container**. Cut a piece from an old vinyl shower curtain, stretch it across the top, and attach it with a strong rubber band.

For a water drum, fill **a metal mixing bowl** with water and float a smaller bowl upside down in it. Strike the smaller one.

Two~Headed Drum

For a two-headed drum, remove the top and bottom from the largest **tin can** you can find. Stretch vinyl, canvas, rubber, leather, or chamois over the openings. Stitch around each head. Lash the stitches top to bottom.

Decorate with feathers, ribbons, or beads!

Use a strip of cloth or doubled-over duct tape to make a strap for your drum. **Then go on parade!**

Drumsticks

Different kinds of drumsticks produce different sounds.

Sticks

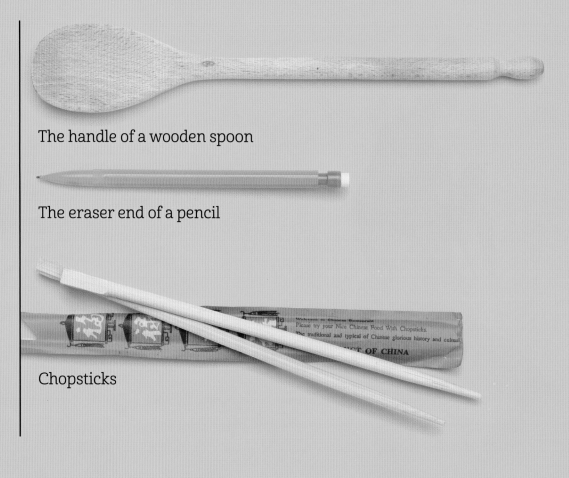

The handle of a wooden spoon

The eraser end of a pencil

Chopsticks

Rods

A bundle of dowels, chopsticks, or straight sticks
secured with rubber bands or electric tape —
have an adult saw off the ends!

Tippers

Use these with frame drums, like the Celtic *bodhran* (BOW-run).

A bubble wand with rubber balls taped on top for weight

Two plastic spoons with their ends taped together

Brushes

The bristles of a paintbrush: brush the drum as though you were painting a picture

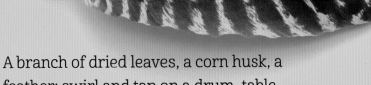

A branch of dried leaves, a corn husk, a feather: swirl and tap on a drum, table, floor, or wooden chair

Fruit Salad

The chart below is a **composition**. Four players each choose a different fruit. Say the name of the fruit in one beat. Then play that rhythm on your instrument. All four players start together on the count of 1 and read across their line, saying or playing the fruit name. ✳ means a beat of silence.

Children's Street Chant

Here's a standard way to **notate**, or write, music.

Say the words first, then play the rhythm on an instrument. This round can have two or more parts, each part entering as the previous part starts the second line.

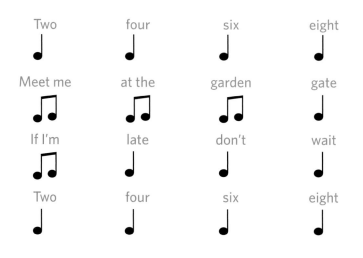

Playing the Room

With two drumsticks or mallets in hand, explore the room, gently striking the floor, the walls, the blinds, the stairs. Tap the chair, the desk, metal cabinets, doorknobs, bottles, wastebaskets, and so on.

Listen to your friends' sounds. Converse with them, varying loud and soft, fast and slow. **Imitate** and **improvise**. Listen — always listen as you play. Record your percussion piece to hear later.

Don't harm or break anything . . . of course!

BUCKET DRUMMING & STOMP

A large, sturdy, 5-gallon bucket makes a faithful drum, played by street musicians in cities worldwide.

For a high sound, hit the bucket's rim.

For a fuller bass sound, try tilting up one side of the bucket with your toes while hitting the center.

Sit on a stool with the bucket between your legs. The stool must be low enough that there's no need to bend over to reach the drum. Hug the bucket with your feet.

Your drum is like a trampoline. Hold your drumsticks between your thumb and pointer finger as you'd hold a pencil: let them bounce off the drum!

Drop the sticks, and use your hands to play the drum! Pick it up and plop it down gently. Slap and knock the sides of it. Pass the buckets in a circle — make up your own patterns!

A drum kit has several drums of different sizes that make different sounds, some high (like a snare drum), some deep (like a bass drum). For a basic drum kit beat, try this rhythm for both hands.

🥁 = Bass

🥁 = Snare

Left	🥁		🥁		🥁		🥁	
Right	🥁	🥁	🥁	🥁	🥁	🥁	🥁	🥁

The percussion ensemble **Stomp** mixes everyday objects with rhythms and movement. They use brooms, metal trash cans, and even match-boxes to create incredible soundscapes.

Percussion Conversations

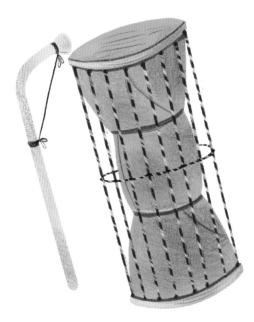

Drums are very chatty instruments; we just need to learn their language. The Nigerian drummer tucks his drum under his arm, squeezing and relaxing the pressure on the leather thongs to raise or lower the pitch. His other hand strikes the drumhead with a curved stick. He converses with other drummers, changing pitches and pulses — sometimes across long distances.

Use instruments instead of words to talk back and forth with a friend; always listen to your partner as you **improvise** and respond.

Nigerian drummer **Aralola Olamuyiwa** gives students talking drums for a class at a school in Lagos. The West African talking drum had in the past served as a means of communication between villages long before the existence of phones. From the way the drum is beaten, those familiar with it can tell if it is announcing a birth, death, marriage, declaration of war, or arrival of the king.

Discover all the ways you can use your hands: tapping, clicking, rolling, knocking, scratching, flicking; using the fingertips, fingernails, wrists, fists, knuckles, and palms. Play on the frame as well as on the drumskin. Just like with speech, you can be loud or quiet, slow or fast, high or low, funny or angry.

Tap it!

Knock it!

Copycat Rhythms

Someone plays a rhythm pattern. Others copy — take turns — follow the leader. Include silence among your sounds. *Listen.*

Scratch it!

Flick it!

At right, a musician plays a set of half-gallon paint cans with mallets during a performance conducted by **John Cage**.

Silence is a vital part of music. John Cage wrote a piece for piano entitled "4'33"," which is exactly 4 minutes and 33 seconds of silence — that's all! It has been performed many times all over the world.

John Cage also wrote a piece for three drums played very softly with the fingertips. You have to listen very carefully to hear it well! Try making up your own piece that sounds mysterious and quiet, then suddenly grows funny and playful, then gradually returns to that mysterious feeling.

Tambourine

Use a tambourine to summon a windy day or a babbling brook.

Hoops

Make hoops of cardboard, heavy belt leather, or flexible plastic. Two paper plates stuck face-together will do in a pinch.

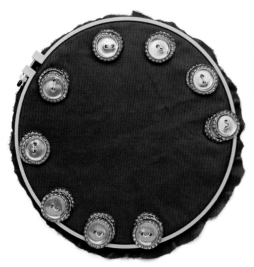

Head

To make a tambourine head, stretch thin hide, rubber inner tubing, canvas, or fabric over a hoop. (After fabric is stretched over the hoop, saturate it with diluted white glue to give the head a better tone and tightness.)

Clappers

Make clappers out of seashells, screw eyes, buttons, washers, coins with holes, or bottle caps flattened with a hammer. Have an adult drill or poke holes in the hoop. Thread clappers or tie them on.

Try embroidery hoops. Stretch the head over the smaller hoop, and secure with the larger hoop. In each of the bottle caps, poke two holes. Thread them onto the head.

Miss Bessie Jones was a song leader who led the traditional call-and-response songs of the Georgia Sea Islands. The tambourine's rhythm filled the room, singers, and dancers with joy and energy. It was also a way of keeping all the singers in time.

For the French horn,
see page 74.

Breath Music
The Winds

The wind whispering in the trees, a train roaring through a tunnel, a friend who whistles while she works — all these sounds are like instruments that make tones by vibrating air.

From quiet to loud, simple to elaborate, these instruments all need air to move through them in order to make music.

Comb Kazoo

Cut a piece of wax paper to the same length as a comb, and twice as wide. Fold the paper over the teeth of the comb, and place the tooth side gently between your lips. You can also try placing it against your lips. Hum or sing a song, and adjust your lips until the buzzing tickles too much to bear!

Wind Tube

Different lengths of plastic pool tubing (1" diameter) seem to sing many notes when swung quickly around and around.

Homemade French Horn

Plastic funnel →

Flexible tubing →

Attach a plastic funnel and trumpet mouthpiece to either end of a yard of shower hose or flexible tubing. Blow into the mouthpiece, buzzing with your lips to make a good sound. Ann heard someone play "Joy to the World" on this tube!

Trumpet mouthpiece

FLUTES, WHISTLES & PIPES

Pipes, whistles, and flutes can be made out of bamboo, cane, plastic drinking straws, garden hose, papier-mâché, and empty ballpoint pen tubes.

Primitive pipes came in all sizes with unscaled notes. With that freedom, you can explore any sound that **tickles the ears.**

Ballpoint pen flutes

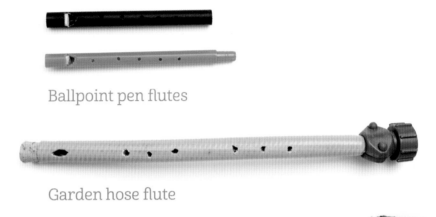

Garden hose flute

Bamboo flute

The **shakuhachi** is a bamboo flute that has been played in Japan and China since ancient times. Unlike a recorder or orchestra flute, the shakuhachi has no mouthpiece, and the musician controls the loudness, sharpness, and softness of the sound by blowing air in different ways. Hundreds of different sounds are possible.

Random Pipes

When you listen to recorded music, join right in with your pipes or another favorite instrument.

Straw Pan Pipes

1. Cut a bunch of plastic straws into different lengths or use ½"–¾" plastic tubing or cane cut in random lengths.

2. Plug the bottoms of the tubes with nondrying modeling clay — the higher you put the plug, the higher the note. (Push in the plug with a pencil or dowel.) To tune the notes better, you can adjust the clay plug.

3. Lash pipes together with string, tape, or shoelace.

PIPE MEASUREMENTS
If you want to get close to a standard Western scale, try:

NOTE	LENGTH
do	12"
re	11"
mi	10"
fa	10"
so	9"
la	9"
ti	8"
do	8"

Long tubes = low notes

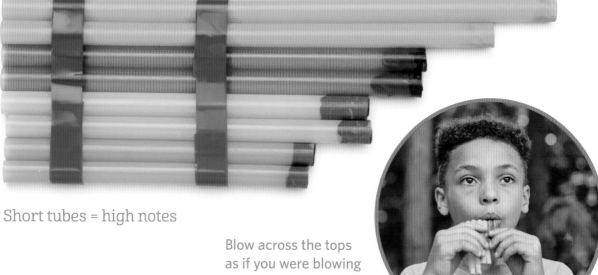

Short tubes = high notes

Blow across the tops as if you were blowing across the top of a bottle. (It takes a little practice.)

Hose Pipes

1. With scissors, cut three pieces of garden hose, each 5" long.

2. Plug one piece with modeling clay at end. Plug second piece at 4" length. Plug third piece at 3" length. (Use a pencil to push in the clay.)

3. Lay pipes on two strips of masking tape. Put a pinch of clay between each pipe. Then wrap tape around. Blow across the top.

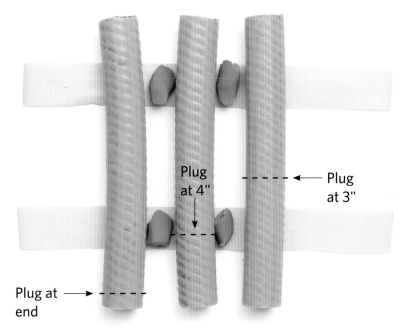

Plug at 4"

Plug at 3"

Plug at end

Box Pipes

Try diminishing sizes of plastic straws. Stick straws in a section of corrugated box. Glue straws in place. Tape bottoms shut, or plug with modeling clay.

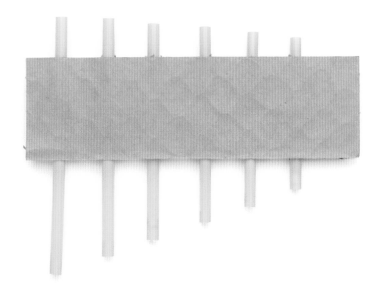

Test Tube Pipes

Vary the amounts of water to create different tones. (Add food coloring so young kids can play a tune by reading a color chart.)

Mark Stewart's Wind Section

Composer and multi-instrumentalist Mark Stewart plays the guitar for a living but has a passion for inventing and sharing new instruments. Here are a few of his creations.

The Chaladoo uses PVC pipe and a clarinet mouthpiece and can be played two ways: either through the mouthpiece as a low clarinet, or through the other airhole as a didgeridoo (an indigenous Australian instrument).

The Slide Whistle Organ uses plastic tubing to link slide whistles, allowing the musician to play multiple whistles at once.

Powered by bicycle, the Velophone spins whirly tubes around to capture the sounds of the wind. A pedal-powered wind organ!

Chaladoo

Slide Whistle Organ

Velophone

Shepherd's Pipe

This pipe is like ones played by shepherds. An adult should help with this project. Use a section of bamboo about 11" long × ⅞" in diameter, or try plastic pipe or a papier-mâché tube formed around a broomstick. Drill finger holes as shown. Don't forget the wind hole near the top on the front and the thumb hole on the back, directly behind the top finger hole.

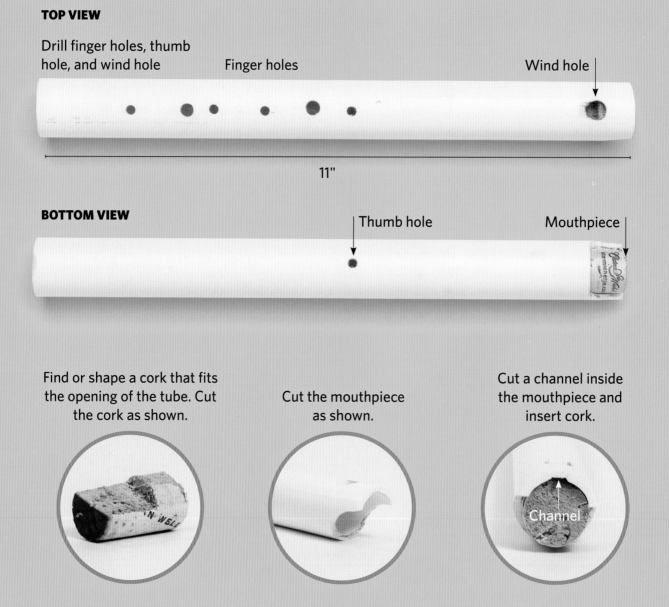

TOP VIEW

Drill finger holes, thumb hole, and wind hole

Finger holes

Wind hole

11"

BOTTOM VIEW

Thumb hole

Mouthpiece

Find or shape a cork that fits the opening of the tube. Cut the cork as shown.

Cut the mouthpiece as shown.

Cut a channel inside the mouthpiece and insert cork.

Channel

ACORN WHISTLES

This autumn, pick up an empty acorn cap. With a little practice, you can make an excellent shrill call. It'll come in handy if you ever feel lost!

Hold the acorn cap with the inside facing you. Create a small, downward-pointing triangle between your thumbs.

Blow directly into the triangle. Keep adjusting the air flow and the triangle size until you get a satisfying, sharp whistle.

Placement of acorn cap

DANDELION TRUMPETS

Why are people so mean to dandelions? We think them beautiful and wild, and they can make MUSIC. We once had a small family orchestra playing Beethoven's "Ode to Joy" on dandelions!

1. Find a long (5" or taller), strong, fat dandelion stem.

2. Snip off the flower.

3. Split the top of the stem with your thumbnail.

4. Pinch the top of the stem to make a flat mouthpiece.

5. Nick finger holes with your finger-nail to make different pitches.

6. Blow with lips closed.

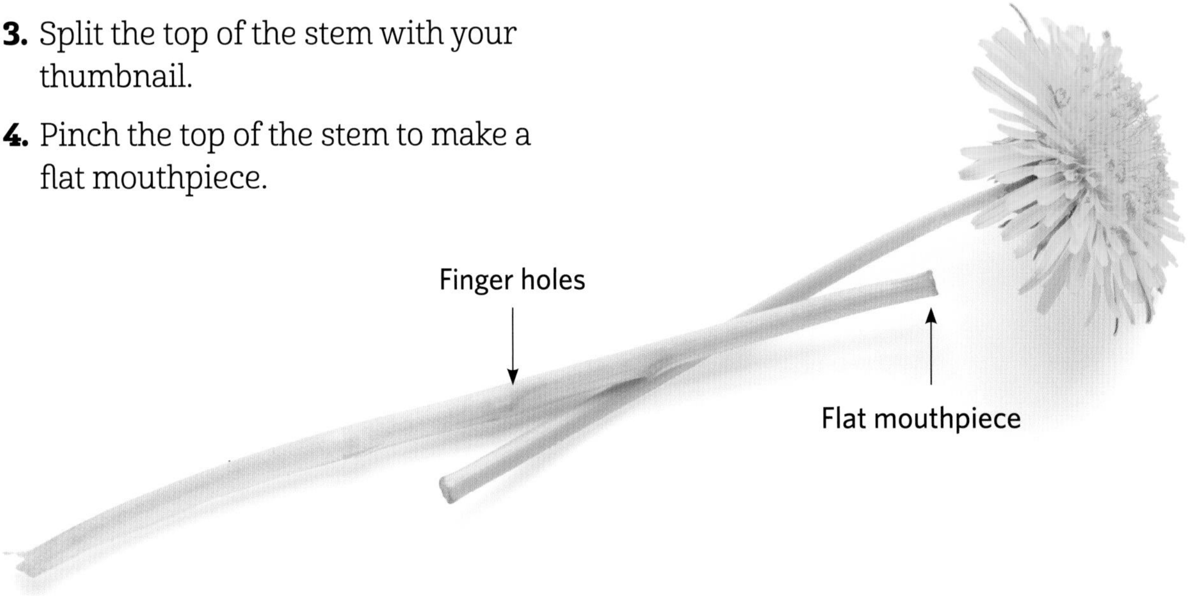

Finger holes

Flat mouthpiece

If you can't make a sound at first, put a little more of the stem into your mouth (up to an inch) or shorten the stem. Buzz with your lips until you get a good sound. The dandelion may last an hour before it wilts.

Soundscapes

You've **seen** a landscape — what about a soundscape you can **hear**?
Let instruments tell the story of a storm or a summer meadow, going
from stillness to sound and back to stillness. Like this . . .

The Rainstorm

Try this game from South Africa with a group of 5 or 50 people, standing together in a line. Start and finish in silence. The person at one end starts the first sound, the next person picks it up, and it continues down the line in a wave. Before the wave reaches the end, the first person starts the next sound, and the wave continues, finally subsiding to quiet again.

Begin in **silence**.
Blow softly with lips: **wind**
Snap fingers, first slow, then fast: **raindrops**
Slap thighs, first slow, then fast: **heavy rain**
Clap hands and stomp feet: **thunder**
Slap thighs, first fast, then slow: **heavy rain**
Snap fingers, first fast, then slow: **raindrops**
Blow softly with lips: **wind**
End in **silence**.

Choose a story to tell in sounds. Create your own soundscape with
instruments and objects, clapping hands, and imaginative voices.

Echoing Nature

Mimicry (MIM-ick-ree) is when one thing copies another's sound. Try mimicking these sounds.

wind: thin-rimmed glass
wailing wind: handsaw with bow
rain: Thimble Fingers (see page 36)
heavy rain: slung mugs (see page 34)
bell buoy: triangle
deep sea, distant thunder: large PVC thumping pipes
insects: guiro, maracas, or shaker
spring peepers and tree frogs: small bells
woodpecker: wood block

Compose a piece about the flight of a paper airplane, or about a porcupine in an inflatable bounce house.

Pictures full of lines, shapes, and colors, like this one by artist Kazimir Malevich, also make great soundscapes. What does a line of small loops sound like? A series of dots or triangles?

The String Section

Pluck and strum, bow and frail!

Early instrument strings were made from animal intestines (called "gut") or silk. Nowadays strings are often made of nylon or metal.

THE SOUNDING BOX

When making stringed instruments, resting them on a hollow **sounding box** while playing will allow them to resonate more freely, giving them a better tone. This is why many stringed instruments, such as a guitar or violin, have a sounding box built in.

Sounding box

SIDE VIEW OF ACOUSTIC GUITAR
The sounding box is built in so the sound resonates when you pluck the strings.

SIDE VIEW OF ELECTRIC GUITAR
Electric guitars send vibrations to an amplifier or "amp," which uses electricity to make them louder. No sounding box is needed, which is why they are flat.

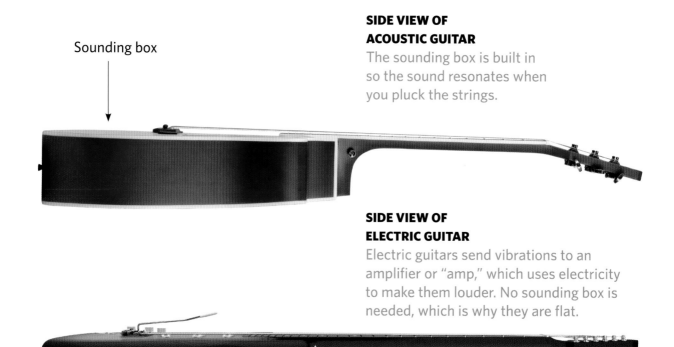

Experiment with this: take a monochord (see page 92), and play it on different surfaces: a wooden box, the floor, a carpet, the ground outside. Where is the sound most clear?

Appalachian Strings

In Kentucky, Virginia, West Virginia, Tennessee, North Carolina, and other states in the Appalachian Mountains, people have made their own instruments for generations using whatever materials they have on hand.

A **washtub bass** is made from a wooden pole, a piece of rope, and a washtub as a sounding box.

Mountain dulcimers, long, boxy instruments with three or four strings, are often made of scrap wood and may use wire staples as frets. Musicians pluck them by hand or strum them with picks — or even feather quills.

Banjos, which descend from West African instruments, have been made from animal hides stretched over metal hoops, cookie tins, and even hubcaps.

This banjo is made with a frying pan, a length of wood, and some strings.

The Rubber Band Band

Here is an oldie-but-goodie of the homemade string section: the rubber-band-jo! Rubber bands sing across a firm box. Try lifting the bridge or pressing more firmly on the strings to get a different set of notes.

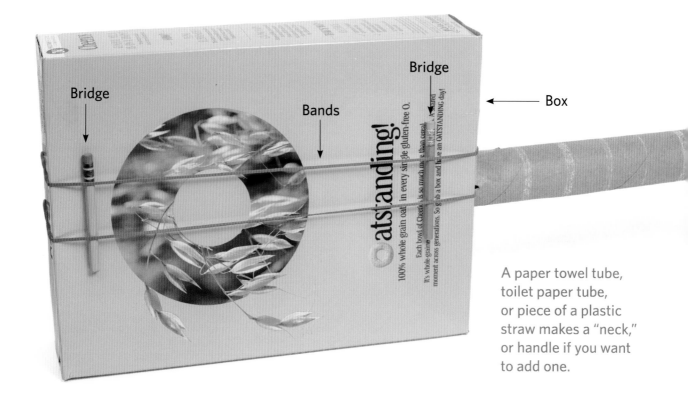

A paper towel tube, toilet paper tube, or piece of a plastic straw makes a "neck," or handle if you want to add one.

Here's a "formula" for constructing rubber band instruments.

BOX	BRIDGE	BANDS
Cereal box	1 or 2 pencils	Thick bands
Tissue box	Cardboard "tent"	Thin bands
Matchbox	Piece of wood	Loose bands
Duct tape roll	Piece of tubing	Tight bands

Monochord
THE HARMONY OF THE SPHERES

A monochord is part music, part mathematics, part magic. The ancient Greeks discovered that they could create the first five notes of a scale, perfectly tuned, by moving a bridge under the string. When the string was divided in specific places, "cutting" it into halves or thirds, they plucked it and heard the notes of the scale. These were called **harmonics**, moving in relation to one another like the planets in outer space.

1. Begin with a hollow wooden box or board.

2. Hammer a nail halfway into one end of the box, and twist a screw eye into the other.

3. String fishing line tightly between both ends (a screw eye can be tightened using a screwdriver as a lever).

4. Insert a small piece of wood or a paper cup as a bridge. You may want two bridges.

2,500 years ago, the Ancient Greeks were exploring the sounds you can make when you pluck a string. A shorter string makes a higher sound, and a longer string makes a lower one.

If using a cup for a bridge, poke holes near the bottom of the cup and string the fishing line through.

String fishing line tightly from screw eye to nail.

Nail

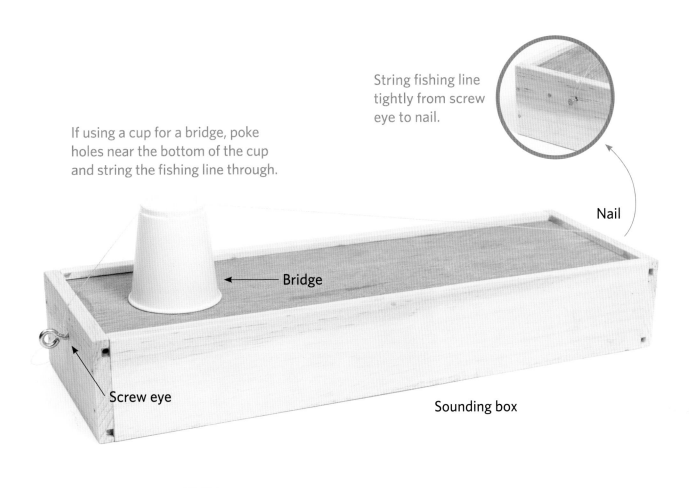

Bridge

Screw eye

Sounding box

Try sliding a second cup up and down the sounding box for different notes.

Pluck or strike the string and listen to its sound. Using a ruler and your ears, find the place where the note is the same on either side of the bridge, known as **sweet**. Can you find other places where the notes on both sides sound sweet, or the same?

Single~Note Compositions

Make up a musical piece using only one note. How will you start? What will happen? How will your single-note piece end?

You can do this on any instrument, or try this. Stretch a big elastic band across the knobs of a chair. Strum the string. Repeat the note, soft and loud, slow and fast. Make spaces of silence between notes.

This can be one of the most difficult things for a composer or a musician: to take **one note** and make it **interesting**.

THE SIMPLE BOARD ZITHER

The zither is a cousin of the guitar, the autoharp, and the mountain dulcimer, and different versions appear in both ancient and modern cultures all over the world. As the strings on a zither get shorter, their sound gets higher in pitch. Although it is easy to play, it can make complex and beautiful music. An adult should help with this project.

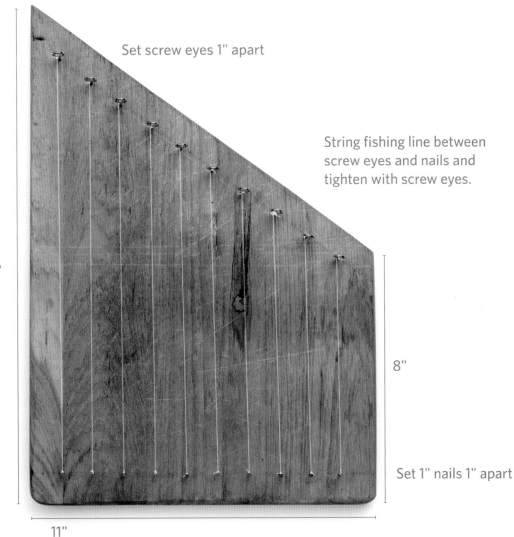

Set screw eyes 1" apart

String fishing line between screw eyes and nails and tighten with screw eyes.

16"

8"

11"

Set 1" nails 1" apart

THE BOX ZITHER

To play a zither, set it flat on a table or hold it on your lap. You can pluck the strings, strum them, stroke them with a violin bow, or strike them with a special light hammer. An experienced adult should lead this project.

1. Make a thin wooden box with an angled edge (16" × 11" × 8") as a sounding box. Use resonant wood like cherry, redwood, maple, cedar, or spruce for the top. The rest of the box can be anything you have handy, like pine.

2. Cut a sound hole approximately 3" in diameter in the lower center of the box. Cut two strips of wood — a 13½" strip for the top to hold the screw-eye string tighteners and an 11" strip for the bottom string holder.

3. Glue strips to the sounding board.

4. String with guitar gut, fishing line, or nylon monofilament. Ten strings are enough, set 1" apart starting 1" from the end.

5. Space the bottom nails, and then use a square to mark the eyebolt holes, then predrill. Use a piece of wood to set nail heights the same.

6. Tune by turning the screw eyes and comparing the sound to the notes of a piano. (Note: be careful not to turn the screw eyes too tightly or the strings may break.)

Guqin

The earliest known surviving instrument of the zither family is a Chinese guqin (pronounced GEE-oo-kin). A seven-stringed zither, the guqin has been played since ancient times and is still a favorite classical instrument in China today.

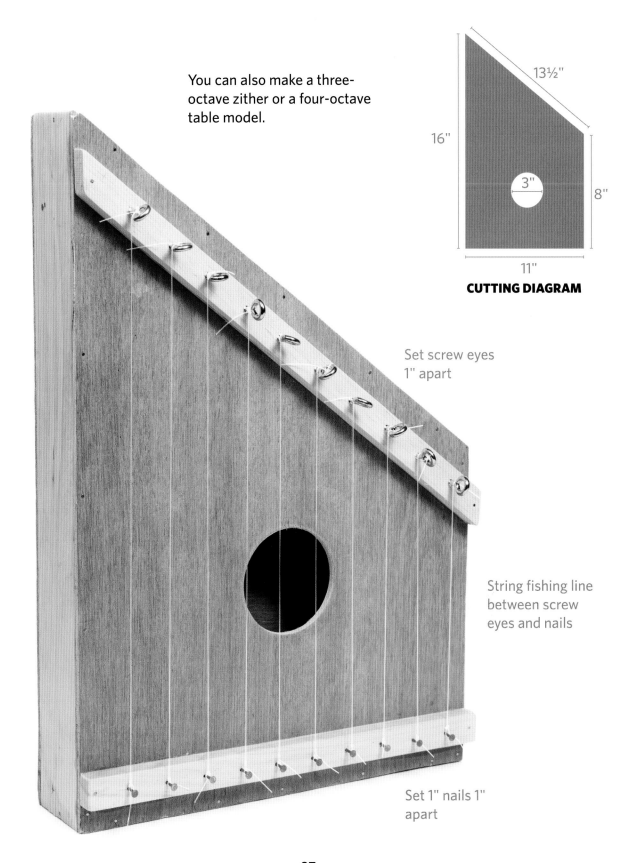

You can also make a three-octave zither or a four-octave table model.

13½"

16"

3"

8"

11"

CUTTING DIAGRAM

Set screw eyes 1" apart

String fishing line between screw eyes and nails

Set 1" nails 1" apart

One~String Box Bass

An experienced adult should lead the way with this project. Here's how one woodworker built the one-string box bass, using a wooden box, a bridge, a stick, a lever, and a guitar string.

1. Make a thin wooden box (8" wide × 12" tall × 3" deep). Use resonant wood like cherry, redwood, maple, cedar, or spruce for the top. The rest of the box can be anything you have handy, like pine.

2. Make a bridge, cutting a slot for the string, and glue to the box top.

3. Cut a sound hole approximately 2¼" in diameter.

4. Cut a 30" stick, which will extend 6" below the box and 12" above it to form a neck. Cut a slot for a snug-fitting lever and drill holes for attaching the lever. Drill a hole for attaching the peg.

5. Cut holes in the top and bottom of the box for the stick neck to pass through *tightly*.

6. Cut a lever, and drill one hole in it for the bolt and one for the string. Attach to the stick neck with a bolt.

7. Attach guitar string or fishing line from lever to peg.

TOP VIEW

SIDE VIEW

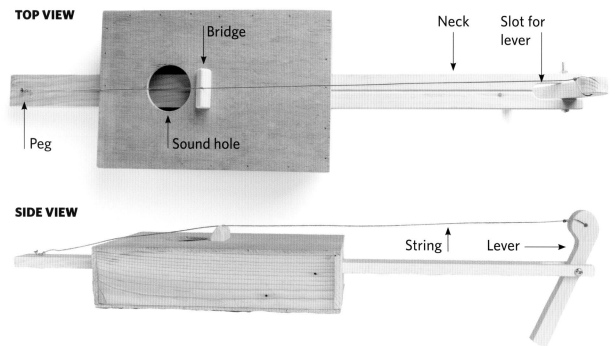

Bridge

Neck

Slot for lever

Peg

Sound hole

String

Lever

Pull down lever handle to change pitch and pluck with fingers or use a bow for different sounds.

An adult should help with this project.

1. Cut an H-shaped hole the width of your stick in the milk carton about 1" from the "roof."

2. Cut slots for strings.

3. Attach three screw eyes to each end of a flat stick or yardstick. Tie each string tightly to one screw eye, pass it through the slot, and tie it to the opposite screw eye. If needed, add a piece of wood on each end of the yardstick to keep screw eyes from poking out the bottom when tightened.

To play: strum, tap, or use an old violin bow.

Slots to hold strings

If you cut this shape in the milk carton, it will hold the stick more tightly when you poke it through.

The screw eyes provide a way to tighten the strings.

Tip: To keep a knot in fishing line from slipping, dot it with superglue.

Many people in the world today make stringed instruments from **recycled** materials.

The Recycled Orchestra of Cateura is an ensemble from Paraguay that has traveled the world playing classical, traditional, and heavy metal music on instruments made from scrap from the junkyard in their city. These playable violins, violas, and cellos are played just like wooden instruments.

The Garbage-Men is a rock band of teenagers from Sarasota, Florida, who perform on homemade instruments, including electric guitars and basses made from cereal boxes, to raise awareness about sustainable living. By attaching a pickup microphone to your instrument and plugging it into an amp, you can make an electric guitar, too.

Musical Saw

The common house saw (for cutting wood) makes beautiful music when a bow is drawn against the toothless edge. As you raise and lower the blade, it makes high and low sounds.

Ann ordered a toothless saw directly from the manufacturer (check on the Internet). The sound is the same, with teeth or without.

Ann's father once played his musical saw in Steinway Hall in New York City. The reviewer said Mr. Wiseman played his "utensil" with skill. It was a voice and piano piece with saw **obligato** (accompaniment).

It's best to use an old violin bow, if you can find one. A bow is very difficult to make, requiring 50 to 100 strands of linen thread, monofilament, or hairs from a horse tail, knotted at both ends. You can buy **rosin** at most music stores to rub on bow strings to make them sing.

1. Place the saw handle flat on your thigh, so the smooth edge of the blade faces away from you.

2. Cross your other leg over to clamp the saw firmly.

3. Place your thumb about 3" from the tip and bend an S curve in the saw blade. Raise the blade up and down, changing the curve in the saw until you find the sounds you want.

4. To play, stroke the saw edge firmly with a violin bow, or draw the bow hard against the curved blade. The voice of the blade is better in certain areas.

5. If you don't have a violin bow, you can tap with a stick as you raise the blade up and down, but you'll get no vibration.

6. The sound varies with the pressure of the bow stroke. A 28" saw will give six or seven notes; a 30" saw will give a full octave, the eight notes of do-re-mi-fa-so-la-ti-do.

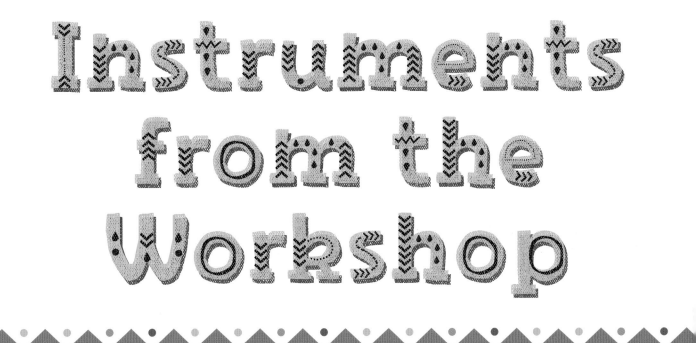

Instruments from the Workshop

Make the instruments in this section with an adult. When working with tools, wear gloves and goggles to protect your fingers and eyes.

Sometimes, making an instrument requires a surprising amount of noise: hammering, sawing, tapping. Be sure to wear ear protection if it gets loud!

Rainstick

Rainsticks are often made of cactuses: the needles are removed from the dry cactus, then driven back into it like nails. Its soothing, watery sound is believed to help bring rain.

1. Poke nails all the way into a PVC tube. Draw holes with a pencil before you try to nail through the tube.

2. Seal one end with a PVC plug or heavy tape and fill the tube a third to halfway full with rice, dried peas, pebbles, or sand.

3. Seal the other end of the tube.

Hand-painted rainsticks from Ecuador

Give your rainstick some color by covering it with decorative tape!

Tongue Drum

Every wood has its own sound. Tap a few boards, and listen. Try spruce, fruit, and redwood for the best sounds. At least make the top out of resonant wood — the rest can be pine.

There is no magic to these measurements — use what you have on hand. A small box will sound higher; a large box will sound deeper and richer. The end piece should be the same height as the sides, and the width should be the width of the top minus a double thickness of the wood used on the sides.

1. Cut two sections of piece **A**, 6" × 26" (sides).

2. Cut two sections of piece **B**, 6" × 8" (ends).

3. Cut piece **C** (top) out of a hardwood (such as redwood), 8" × 26".

4. Cut **bottom** from anything, 8" × 26".

5. Drill starting holes and then insert the coping saw blade to make the slits.

6. Cut six tongues into the top, each a different length and width.

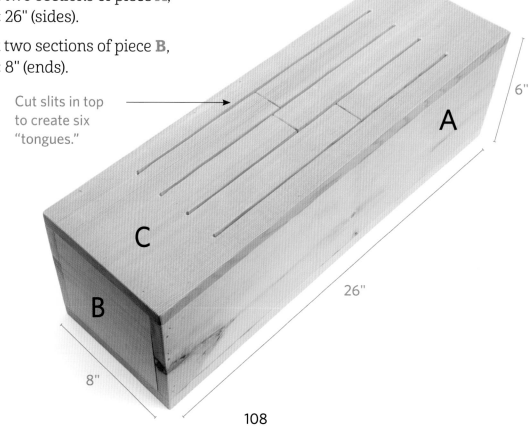

Cut slits in top to create six "tongues."

For mallets,
see page 33.

WINDOW WIND HARP

Could this be the sound of the ancient Aeolian harp?
Aeolus was the Greek god of the winds.

1. Make a box as wide as your window.

2. Put 6–10 screw eyes along one end, and drill a corresponding number of holes along the other end.

3. Tie (or melt with a match) a long piece of fishing line around the screw eye closest to you, weave it through the matching hole, then back through the next screw eye. Continue until the fishing line is threaded through the entire instrument.

4. Make two 1" bridges and place them under the strings to tighten. (If you can tune the strings to exactly the same pitch, a strong wind will give you the great harmonic sound of the spheres.)

5. Set the harp in your window on a windy day, half in and half out, to catch the breeze.

6. Let the window frame hold it in place. Listen to the song of the wind.

bridge

bridge

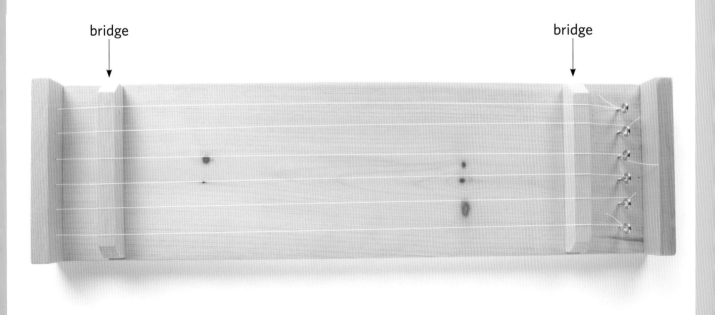

111

Wooden Xylophone

Some kinds of wood can really sing. Hard, resonant woods, such as redwood and fruitwood, make the best tones, but you may have to have them specially cut. Pine is less resonant, but much easier to find. An experienced adult should lead this project.

1. Cut ¾" board into ⅞" strips. Cut eight or more pieces at different lengths for different pitches (see chart).

2. Tuning can be random or scaled. These measurements are approximate. To make a note higher, sand or saw off a sliver from the end. To lower a note, saw a shallow notch into the block.

3. Make a rack to hold the note bars out of wood or Styrofoam or two lengths of felt weather stripping on a flat surface. If you use wood for the rack, line it with felt strips as shown for stability and resonance.

4. Do not glue the note bars onto the rack. The bars must be free in order to ring and release their sound.

BAR MEASUREMENTS

NOTE	LENGTH
high so	6¾"
high fa	7⅛"
high mi	7⅜"
high re	7¾"
high do	8⅜"
ti	8½"
la	9¼"
so	9⅝"
fa	10¼"
mi	10¾"
re	11½"
do	12⅛"
low ti	12⅞"
low la	13½"
low so	14¼"

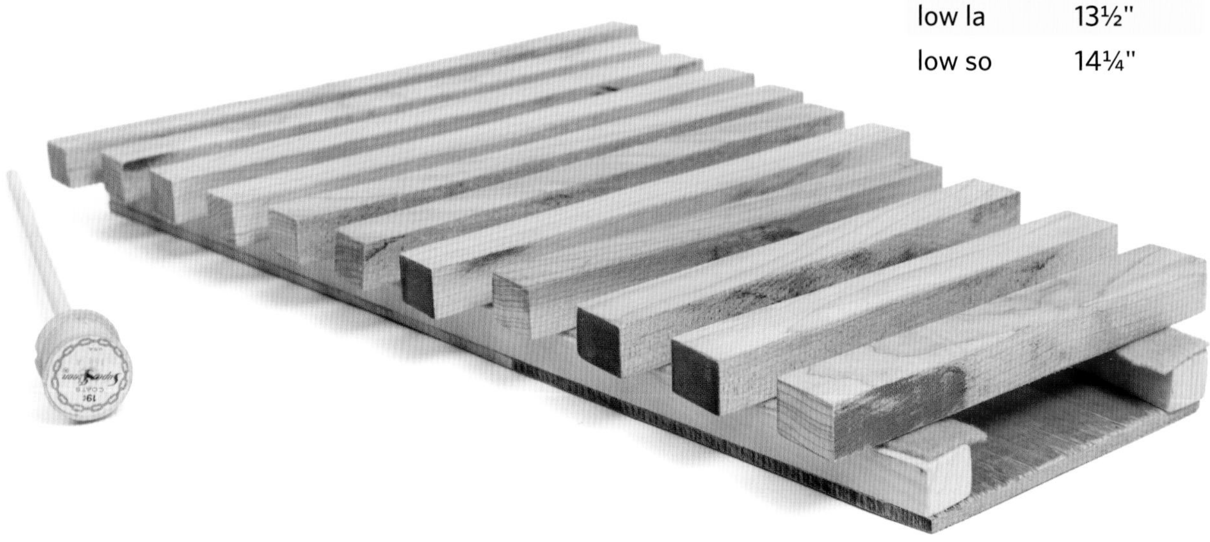

Tuning can be tricky. While you're figuring it out, try playing a set of random notes . . . and invent your own new sounds and scales.

KALIMBA / MBIRA

In Africa, there are dozens of ways to make the kalimba (kuh-LIM-buh), mbira (mm-BEE-ruh), or "thumb piano" — all names for an instrument you can play while sitting, standing, or walking around. Here are just a few.

Cigar Box Mbira

To make the **tongues**, or finger pegs, have an adult hammer umbrella spokes, flatten coat hanger wire of different lengths, or flatten "cut nails." Use two small strips of wood for bridges. Lash a short pencil or dowel in place with wires.

Poke the wires through the box lid, securing them on the other side of the lid under a glued-on strip of wood if needed.

Tongue Depressor Mbira

For this mbira you need seven tongue depressors and some strong glue. Sandwich five tongue depressors between the other two, arranging them so they protrude at different lengths to make different pitches. Glue to secure.

Coconut Shell Mbira

In tropical parts of Africa, thumb pianos are made with smoothed coconut shells. They are beautiful but are tricky to create.

Some African musicians will walk for miles while quietly playing the kalimba to themselves.

Shingle Plunker

Here is another way to make a thumb piano.

1. Sand a shingle smooth. (Cedar is best.)

2. Cut it in half with a coping saw or an X-Acto knife.

3. In the thinner half, cut slits in diminishing lengths to form teeth.

4. This will be the top piece. Nail two thin strips of wood to the thicker end of the other piece of shingle.

5. Nail the thin top piece to the cross bars as shown.

Clock Music Opus 3
ANYTHING GOES

On this score you can substitute other instruments for the ones listed.

▥ = seedpods,
maracas, shakers

▲ = drum
(only one beat)

● = claves, guiro,
seashells

★ = bells

◆ = kalimba,
glockenspiel, xylophone

❱ = rainstick
(let fall only once)

✳ = triangle, cowbell
(one tap)

♟ = gong, cymbal
(with one soft stick)

Now make up your
own scores and
play them with your
friends.

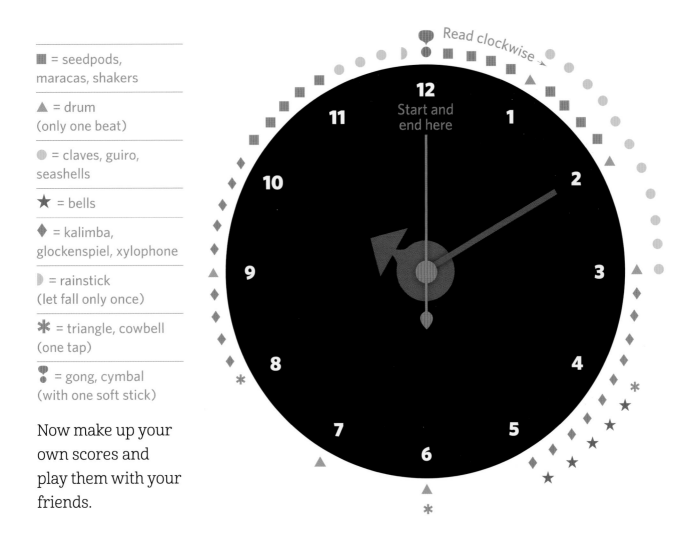

Creating Music

Even without making instruments, you have plenty of ways and tools to bring music to life. Follow your curiosity when making music, and don't be afraid to imagine new possibilities — and to practice until you can play what you hear in your head.

Here are some games, ideas, and prompts to help you create music from and for the world around you.

Scores

A **score** is a set of musical instructions written on paper. You can make your own score to help you and others know how to perform your compositions. What shapes and designs remind you of certain sounds?

Maybe ∼∼∼∼ means "a low rumble."

Maybe ❋ means "a long, beautiful note on a flute."

Use symbols to represent musical sounds — make sure it's clear what order to play the sounds in — and then perform.

You can also make a score using a clock: check out pages 15, 39, 117!

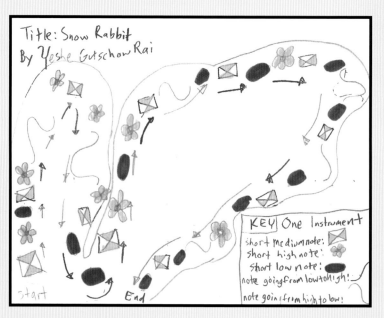

Composer John Cage drew scores for several pieces, including *Cartridge Music*.

Scores Outdoors

Outside on a snowy winter day, find a patch of snow with no footprints. Create a musical score by leaving different kinds of tracks in the snow, then follow your footprints back while playing an instrument. Or "read" your score and play it through a window!

Try this at the beach or with chalk on a sidewalk.

IMAGINING AND INVENTING NEW INSTRUMENTS

People have had different reasons to create new instruments. Sometimes, they needed to make a certain sound that no existing instrument could make. Other times they only had limited materials.

Anything you can make vibrate will sound. So how will your new instrument vibrate?

Will it…

…have strings, like a guitar or a violin?

…have something stretched over it that you hit, like a drum?

...be blown into, like a flute or horn?

... be hit with a mallet, like a xylophone?

... be shaken, like a rattle or a rainstick?

The trick, really, is to **follow your ears**. What sounds would you like to hear together?

Can your instrument be played in more than one of these ways? A banjo, for instance, can be played by hitting the head like a drum or by strumming like a guitar.

Look at the materials you have on hand. Can you invent an instrument using what's around you?

Paints, colorful balloons, buttons, ribbons, stickers, and markers are all ways to give your instrument its own style.

The Baschet Brothers' Inventions

Playing the **Cristal Baschet**, invented by two brothers in France, is similar to rubbing your finger along the wet rim of a wine glass. Instead, you run your fingertips along wet glass tubes.

The brothers also invented an **inflatable guitar**, which would be convenient for traveling. See how blue it is!

An Instrument You Can Play by Waving at It

The **theremin** is an electronic instrument that is played by moving your hands closer to and farther away from two antennae.

At left, Alexandra Stepanoff plays the theremin on NBC Radio in July 1930. She was taught by the Russian inventor and physicist Léon Theremin.

Recording and Sharing Your Sounds

A microphone is an instrument. Just as a guitar turns touch into sound, a microphone turns sound into electric signals that can be recorded. Microphones are built into our world: into computers, smartphones, cameras, speakers, and even some cars! Yes, it's strange that we can record each other at any time, but this technology also means that it's easy to capture musical compositions to play back and share.

Try recording the music you make into a phone or computer's built-in recording software and playing it back. When you play it back, can you make yourself forget that it's you who's playing? What do you *hear*?

You can even play along with the recording of yourself, or add new layers of recordings on different instruments. Then you can share your recordings with friends.

THE FOUND SOUND MIXTAPE

Find a way to make a recording: with a small digital recorder, a smartphone, an old tape recorder, or a laptop computer with a microphone. Record 10 things that are making sound around your home and outside. Try not to include voices. Play the sounds for friends and family without saying what they are. Can anyone guess?

You can also try recording a sound for a few minutes, then singing or playing along with it on another instrument.

Old-time storytelling radio shows used many found sounds to stir the listener's imagination.

"Listen to everything all the time and remind yourself when you are not listening."
— Pauline Oliveros, composer

Record Your World!

The Internet is a powerful tool for sharing the sounds of your world. On the *MakeMusic4Kids* Facebook page, you can upload the recordings of music you make and listen to other kids' compositions. Let's make some digital noise!

When **Pauline Oliveros** held the microphone of her recorder out the window, she realized the microphone picked up sounds she hadn't noticed were there. There are sounds that exist in the world around us but go unnoticed until we "find" them again. Once you find the sounds around you, how can you make music with them?

Orchestrating

Orchestrate (choose instruments to play) the words of a song or a poem that grows longer and longer. Bring in different body language or percussion instruments to accompany each new addition to this well-known story. Never slow the rhythm. It's tricky!

All instruments
(called *tutti*)

Snapping fingers

Clapping hands

Slapping knees

Rubbing hands

Barking like a dog

Stomping feet

Beating chest

Other pieces that accumulate, or build up, include:
- "This Old Man"
- "The 12 Days of Christmas"
- "The Tree in the Wood"
- "The Rattlin' Bog"
- "Old MacDonald Had a Farm"
- "Chad Gad Yo"
- "Alouette"

This is the house that Jack built.

This is the malt that lay in the house that Jack built.

This is the rat that ate the malt that lay in the house that Jack built.

This is the cat that killed the rat that ate the malt that lay in the house that Jack built.

This is the dog that worried the cat that killed the rat that ate the malt that lay in the house that Jack built.

This is the cow with the crumpled horn that tossed the dog that worried the cat that killed the rat that ate the malt that lay in the house that Jack built.

This is the maiden all forlorn that milked the cow with the crumpled horn that tossed the dog that worried the cat that killed the rat that ate the malt that lay in the house that Jack built.

This is the man all tattered and torn that kissed the maiden all forlorn that milked the cow with the crumpled horn that tossed the dog that worried the cat that killed the rat that ate the malt that lay in the house that Jack built.

Afterward, play this story all the way through on sounds alone, without words. **WOW!**

128

Songwriting

At Norma Jean's home in New England, the chickadee sings even on the deepest wintry days. You too can write a song! Don't worry if it's not as lively as a birdsong; we all must start somewhere.

Like the call of the *chick-a-dee-dee-dee*, your first song can be as simple as a few words. A little boy who once lived here wrote a song which simply goes:

"Sit by the fire with me! Sit by the fire with me!" (Tap the beat on your knees:)

1	2	3	4
Sit	by the	fire	with me!

Some songwriters find it helpful to write with an instrument. Try inventing words while playing one of your homemade instruments, or while keeping a beat with your hands. Does the instrument you're playing sound like a feeling? Some people say the banjo sounds happy, or the bassoon sounds angry.

Find a place or an activity where you like to write songs. Try writing a song on the swing set or on a bicycle, while jumping rope or tossing a ball: these all help you keep the beat.

If you are stuck finding notes to sing, sing it all on one note or chant the words — it's no big deal. You could even borrow a melody from a song you like.

Chick-a-dee-dee-dee-dee

Write songs with your
friends: sit down together,
pat a beat on your knees,
and tell a funny story
together. Rhyming is
optional. Write songs about
your own lives.

Rap and Hip~Hop

Hip-hop, born in the African-American and Latino communities of American cities, is for many people a way of life: music, art, dance, a way of dressing, and a way to share real experiences. Hip-hop music is creative and raw and uses modern technology in many interesting ways:

Scratching is moving a vinyl record back and forth on a turntable to produce a rhythmic sound.

Sampling is taking a small section — a drum beat, baseline, or snippet of song — from another recording and using it as part of your own music.

Rapping is a spoken singing, a kind of chant, which is done over a beat. The roots of rap can be traced back hundreds of years to West African storytellers.

The words we sing have meaning, but we need to remember they also have rhythm and melody. Try writing four lines of poetry and rapping them over a beat. Look at the jump rope chants on page 19 for inspiration.

What do you have to say that needs to be heard?

Notation
WRITING DOWN YOUR RHYTHMS

Here is a way many composers **notate**, or write, rhythms so musicians know how and when to play.

The top number means there are 4 beats to a measure.

Whole note = 4 beats
Half note = 2 beats
Quarter note = 1 beat
Eighth note = Half a beat

A dot adds one-half of the preceding note's time. For example: dotted half = 3 beats

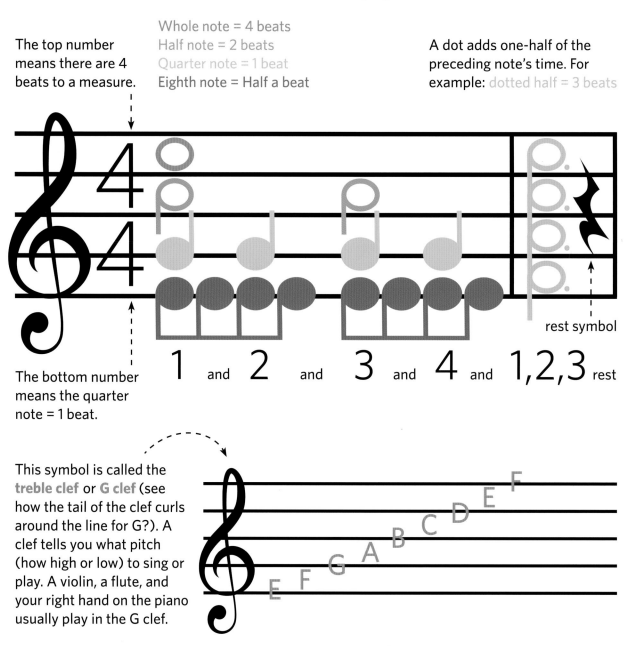

The bottom number means the quarter note = 1 beat.

1 and 2 and 3 and 4 and 1,2,3 rest

rest symbol

This symbol is called the **treble clef** or **G clef** (see how the tail of the clef curls around the line for G?). A clef tells you what pitch (how high or low) to sing or play. A violin, a flute, and your right hand on the piano usually play in the G clef.

MUSIC WITH BABIES AND TODDLERS

Many of the projects in this book can be used to introduce young children to musicmaking. Try activities that combine sound with other sensations, like sight, touch, or movement.

Metal bowls floating in the bathtub chime when they hit one another.

A set of test tubes, or glasses, with varying amounts of water can be tapped to play melodies. Add food coloring so small people can play a tune by reading a color chart.

Begin introducing new music into your life: listen together as a family while cooking or driving. Use some of the recordings in the Resources section of this book (page 138) as a starting point.

Speak or sing a rhyme while bouncing a baby on your knee.

End Notes

From Norma Jean Haynes

There can be such a fine line between making music and living. The air we need to breathe is the same air we use to sing. We use musical words to describe our bodies, and body words to describe our instruments: the heart *beats*, the ears *ring*, the guitar has a *head* and a *neck*. We hold our instruments so near; we vibrate them close to our hearts or between our lips.

We wish for a musical world: a world with more *dynamics* and *harmony,* where *dissonance resolves* and voices can be heard in *unison.* When we lift our pipes, our strings, and our voices to play together, we can experience these ideals as realities.

It takes less than a moment for a thought or a feeling to become music. Keep the pathways for self-expression clear, create spaces where even the quietest among us can be heard, and we can move through the world with newfound joy and reverence.

I hope you take music with you everywhere you go — and I hope you go many places.

From John Langstaff

Toward the end of one of my teaching videos, I ask the children,

"What is music?"

They sit there thinking, silent, as they wonder what I was asking. We had spent two weeks together discovering what pitch, rhythm, dynamics, phrasing, canons, drones, harmony, composing, and conducting meant.

No answer.

I urge them on. "I know you know it! Don't think so hard, just say the first thing that comes into your head! Go back to our earliest thoughts about how music began."

Long pause.

Suddenly a hand flies up above the group, and Rebecca exclaims, "Sound! Sounds."

"Yes," I respond, elated at the answer. Going on (for here was my chance), I ask, "And what is the opposite of sound?"

Not a word, everyone thinking hard. Finally Pedro murmurs, "Quiet?" which prompts another voice to say, "Silence."

"Yes, exactly. That's it!" I say. "You've got it! Sound and silence."

I couldn't have been more pleased.

From Ann Sayre Wiseman

When I think about music, I am amazed at the way it affects people's emotions, how it lets people's feelings out and makes them dance.

When I think about instruments, I see my dad stroking his musical saw, making it cry the mournful tune "Drink to Me Only with Thine Eyes." I see a lonesome man pouring his soul into his mouth organ, cupped between his hands, making it cry and laugh, making it moan. I see the music student I roomed with in Paris years ago hugging her viola da gamba, carrying it all over Paris, strapped to her back. I see my little son, not yet one, with a spoon and a pot making a sound all his own. I see a girl with a tin pennywhistle playing Irish ballads that break your heart at the sound of "Oh Danny Boy, the pipes, the pipes are calling. . . ."

Every spring, a woman sets up her glass harp in Harvard Square, letting spectators turn the wheel as she plays "Jesu, Joy Of Man's Desiring" with her fingers on the wet glass. Nearby, a Chinese man plays a two-string bamboo instrument with a thin bamboo bow, making sounds very foreign to our Western ears. But it's clear he's in love with these sounds, as the strings cry strange notes under his quick strokes.

I think everyone needs an instrument, like an extra voice that lets the feelings out when words are not enough.

I hope when you finish making instruments from these pages that you will find one you love and teach it the language of your heart. Then you will always have a secret friend.

Helpful Musical Terms

Canon. A round; a musical piece in which two or more performers all have exactly the same melody but start at different times

Composer. A person who creates and records new music

Composition. A piece of musical work

Crescendo. Starting soft and growing louder

Diminuendo. Starting loud and growing softer

Dynamics. Loudness and softness

Harmony. Two musical notes that agree with each other when played at once

Imitate. To copy or mimic something else, in this case to mimic its sound

Improvise. To make up (new music) on the spot

Notate. To write out the sounds, pitches, and rhythms of a musical composition so it can be played by others

Opus. One in a series of compositions by a specific composer

Orchestrate. To assign different parts of a piece to different instruments

Polyrhythms. A combination of different rhythms, all played at once

Resonance. How something shakes, or vibrates, while making sound. Every sounding object resonates

Rhythm. A strong, repeated pattern of sounds

Sonic. Related to sound

Syncopation. Temporarily changing the accent in a musical passage to emphasize the weak beat

Tempo. The speed of a piece

Timbre. The texture of a tone: rough or smooth, sharp or sweet

Tone. A single pitch

Unison. All together, as one

Resources

Music for Listening

Having made our own music with this book, we can also hear how some of these same simple ideas are used by composers of sophisticated, serious music. It's easy to locate any of these composers on the Internet and hear some of their pieces online: the Baschet brothers, Luciano Berio, Pierre Boulez, Henry Brant, Earle Brown, Carlos Chavez, Henry Cowell, Meredith Monk, Lou Harrison, Alan Hovhaness, Luigi Nono, Carl Orff, Harry Partch, Gunther Schuller, Karlheinz Stockhausen, and Edgar Varese.

Here are composers and pieces mentioned in this book, as well as some others of interest.

Benjamin Britten. *Noye's Fludde* (1958).

Henry Brant. *Kitchen Music* (1946) and other works. Visit nmbx.newmusicusa.org for a listen.

Carlos Chavez. *Toccata for Percussion Instruments* (1942) and other works.

John Cage. "4'33"" (1952); *Amores* (1943; one movement is for quiet drums).

Franz Josef Haydn. *Symphony no. 47 in G major* (1772). In the third movement, each section of the score is followed by its exact mirror image.

Tim Hazell and *Collar del Viento,* the Children's Pre-Hispanic Orchestra.

Meredith Monk. *Our Lady of Late: Music for Voice and Glass* (1973). Each of these pieces is composed for voice and a crystal wineglass of water.

Wolfgang Amadeus Mozart. *Adagio for Glass Harmonica in C Major* (1791, K. 356; K. 617a); *Adagio and Rondo for Glass Harmonica, Flute, Oboe, Viola, and Cello in C Minor* (1791, K. 617).

Harry Partch. *Cloud-Chamber Music; Ring Around the Moon* (both 1949–50). Numerous works for cloud chamber bowls, gourd tree with gongs, and more.

Karlheinz Stockhausen. *Zyklus for Percussion* (1959). A solo percussion piece for nine instruments. The score is written so that the performance can start on any page, and it can be read upside down, or from right to left, as the performer chooses.

Other Good Resources

Margaret Galloway. *Making and Playing Bamboo Pipes* (Dryad Press, 1963). Instructions on making precise bamboo pipes. Now out of print, but worth a search in a used-book store.

Bart Hopkin. *Making Musical Instruments with Kids* (See Sharp Press, 2009). A creative and easy-to-follow guide from a modern instrument inventor.

Maureen Kenney. *Circle Round the Zero: Play Chants & Singing Games of City Children* (MMB Music, 1975). Great resource on jump rope rhymes and street chants.

Nancy and John Langstaff. *Sally Go Round the Moon* (Revels, 1986). A collection of songs and singing games that can be played on percussion instruments, pitched and nonpitched, some in a single rhythmic pattern (as drone, or *ostinato*), others as melodic lines.

Pauline Oliveros. *Sonic Meditations* (Smith Publications, 1974). A series of listening exercises, some of which will go over well with children. Easily found online.

Ronald Roberts. *Musical Instruments Made to Be Played* (Dryad Press; republished by David & Charles, 1976).

David Rothenberg. *Why Birds Sing* (Basic Books, 2006). A poetic look at the songs of birds and how they have inspired musicians.

Oliver Sachs. *Musicophilia* (Knopf, 2007). Writings on how music affects our brains.

R. Murray Schafer. *The Thinking Ear* (Arcana Editions, 1986). Schafer's writings on music education inform several of our thoughts in this book, and he has been a great inspiration to many musicians and teachers.

Ruth Crawford Seeger. *Animal Folk Songs for Children* (Linnet Books, 1993).

Bryna Stevens. *Ben Franklin's Glass Armonica* (Carolrhoda Books, 1983). Illustrated by Priscilla Kiedrowski. The story of Franklin's fascinating invention.

Ann Sayre Wiseman, *Making Things: The Handbook of Creative Discovery* (Little, Brown & Co., 1997). Dozens of useful and creative projects.

Videos

How to Play the Didgeridoo (Australian Bushcraft Library, 1996). Chris Adnam. P.O. Box 19, Hopetoun Gardens, Elsternwick, Victoria, 3185, Australia; or bushcrft@ozemail.com.au

Landfill Harmonic (Red Antelope Films, 2015). This film follows the Recycled Orchestra of Cateura, Paraguay, as they gain recognition and travel the world.

Let's Sing! (Langstaff Video Project, 1998). John Langstaff teaches children (ages 3 to 7) songs with their own accompanying percussion.

Throw Down Your Heart (The Old School Ltd., New York, and Argot Pictures, 2009). Banjo player Bela Fleck travels through African countries, playing his five-string banjo with traditional and contemporary musicians.

Let's Keep Singing! (University of Washington Music Library, 2017). John Langstaff teaches children (ages 8 to 10) songs with their own accompanying percussion, including clock music.

Stomp Out Loud! (Well Go USA, 1997.). Directed by Luke Cresswell and Steve McNicholas. A video recording of the amazing percussion group that makes music and theater using ordinary found objects.

Websites

Check out this organization of performers, composers, and producers dedicated entirely to "adventurous contemporary music" using ordinary and extraordinary sounds. https://bangonacan.org

Watch videos and learn about musical collaborations between kids around the world, using found sounds and recordings. https://www.foundsoundnation.org

Learn about, listen to, and order a musical saw. www.musicalsaw.com

Site devoted to the glass harmonica or "armonica." www.glassarmonica.com

Wooden parts for instruments. www.amwoodinc.com

Lesson plans, songs to learn, and videos about music traditions from around the world. By Philadelphia-based music teacher Jay Sand. https://www.allaroundthisworld.com

Learn about crankies, moving scrolls that tell stories set to music. www.thecrankiefactory.com

Website of modern Dutch instrument inventor Yuri Landman. www.hypercustom.nl

A performing percussion group that drums on and with ordinary found objects such as hubcaps, pipes, street signs, and plastic garbage pails. https://stomponline.com

The Vegetable Orchestra, based in Vienna, Austria, makes instruments from vegetables (such as a carrot flute), plays them (everything from classical music to traditional African music), and then serves vegetable soup to the audience. www.gemueseorchester.org

Acknowledgments

Ideas, credits, and thanks to: the many people who invented, explored, and created musical instruments at Boston Children's Museum when I was there, and the 1972–73 staff of the Advisory for Open Education in Cambridge, Massachusetts — especially Cornelia Voorhees; the Education Development Center and Dan Watt and Emily Romney of the Elementary Science Study, who conceived *The Musical Instrument Recipe Book* and *Whistles and Strings*, published by McGraw-Hill; Paul Earls, Mariagnese Knill-Cattaneo, and Suzanne Pearce for helpful suggestions. Carl von Mertens for instrument-building help; Mills & Boon Ltd., for permission to reproduce the scale on page 76, from *Making Musical Instruments* by Peter Williams (1973); Albert Whitman & Company for the random pipes made from garden hose described on page 77, adapted from *Music and Instruments for Children to Make* by John Hawkinson and Martha Faulhaber, copyright © 1969 by Albert Whitman & Company.
— **A. S. W.**

Sarah Cantor, David Coffin, Brian Holmes, Shaun Conroy, Tro Langstaff, and Sarah Tenney are friends who came up with answers to my questions.
— **J. L.**

Thanks to Penny Schultz, Chris Haynes, and Diane Sanabria, who brought music to life for me in childhood, and to the many others who have done so since.
— **N. J. H.**

Metric Measurements

1" (inch) = 2.54 centimeters

1 foot = 30.5 centimeters

1 yard = 0.9 meter

1 cup = 0.24 liters

1 gallon = 3.8 liters

Clock Score

Create your own clock score! Photocopy this page, or visit www.storey.com/clock-score to download a printable clock score for composing, orchestrating, and conducting your own original music.

Title of Piece

SOUNDS
Make up a symbol for each sound and list them all here, so you know what is being played when.

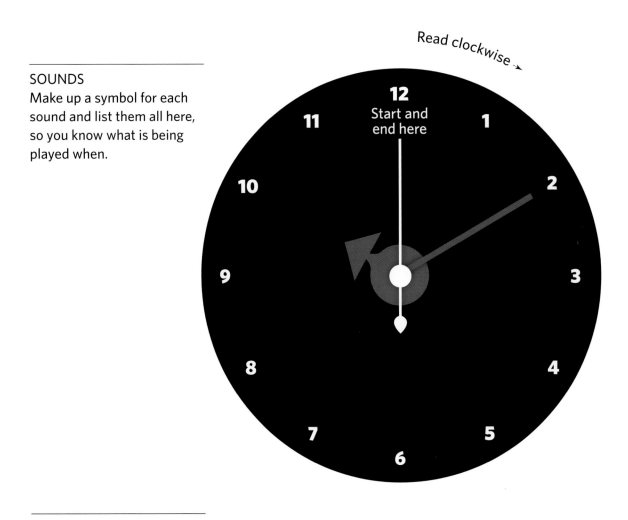

Read clockwise →

Composer

Date

Index

Jump~Start Your Creativity
with More Books from Storey

by Emily K. Neuburger

Make a visual day-in-your-life map, turn random splotches into quirky characters for a playful story, and list the things that make you *you*! These 60 interactive writing prompts and art how-tos will spur your imaginative self-expression.

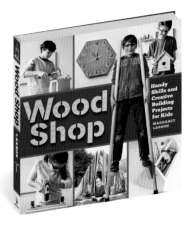

by Nicole Blum & Catherine Newman

Create, hack, or customize! Step-by-step directions show you the basics of how to sew, embroider, knit, crochet, weave, and felt. You can then use your new skills to hand-make cool bracelets, backpacks, merit badges, keychains, and more.

by Margaret Larson

Learn key skills like how to drive a nail and operate a power drill. Then use what you've learned to build 17 fun and creative projects, including your very own workbench, a clever portable tic-tac-toe game, a message board, and more.

Join the conversation. Share your experience with this book, learn more about Storey Publishing's authors, and read original essays and book excerpts at storey.com. Look for our books wherever quality books are sold or call 800-441-5700.